Roadmap to Sust

in Rural Development

All Rights Reserved ©

No part of this publication may be reproduced, stored in a retrieval system, or transmitted in any form or by any means without the author's prior written permission and that of the publisher (2020).

Disclaimer (Exclusive clause)

The author and all employees disclaim any incorrect interpretation, wrong answers to questions or text, harm including emotional, psychological, and physical or any form of the liability to the reader/listener or being given information by third parties.

Furthermore, this disclaimer protects all contributory people, directors, employees, 3rd parties, authors and will not be liable for any injury caused.

Summary   Content

All Right Reserve   1

Disclaimer Exclusive clause   1

Summary Headings   2

Chapters headings (1-13)   3

Dedication   4

Acknowledgement   4

Preface   5

About the Author   7

Details Content   8

Chapter 1:   15

Sustainable agriculture for rural development

Chapter 2:   32

Water management and irrigation techniques

Chapter 3:   42

Agro-ecological practices for rural development

Chapter 4:   55

Technological innovations in sustainable agriculture

Chapter 5:   78

Climate-smart agriculture

Chapter 6:   91

The economic viability of sustainable practices

Chapter 7:   106

Social and cultural dimensions of sustainable
agriculture

Chapter 8:   118

Policies and governance for sustainable rural

agriculture

Chapter 9:   131

Case studies of successful sustainable agriculture

projects

Chapter 10:   147

Future directions for sustainable agriculture in rural

development

Chapter 11:   160

Global and regional policy frameworks for

sustainable development

Chapter 12:   172

Education and capacity building in rural areas

Chapter 13:   184

Rural infrastructure for sustainable development

Reference   207

Glossary   212

Index   255

Dedication

I dedicate this book to my son and my paternal grandmother, Ms. Safoa, who died at the age of 105 years.

Very assertive, methodological and excellent in

Acknowledgement.

As with all the previous one hundred and thirty books I have written and published, I acknowledge the Guardians' help, knowledge, wisdom, and the direction Almighty God has given me to write this book. It would have been impossible to finish writing these books because when I started writing,
I never knew how and when I would end or where to conduct my research, but once I began, I received more and more guidance from Almighty God. With him, this book was written. He directed and gave me the resources; therefore, the real author of this publication is God.
Forgive and love every then, trust, believe and have faith in God. This FORMULA IS THE KEY TO HEAVEN.

PREFACE

Rural development is the continuous and comprehensive socio-economic process of improving rural life. It traditionally focuses on exploiting land-intensive natural resources such as forests and agriculture.

Farming is the fabric of rural society and the main economic activity in many countries. It could severely affect social and political stability in economically developing countries.

Healthy, sustainable, and inclusive food systems are critical to achieving the world's development goals. Agricultural development is one of the most powerful tools for ending extreme poverty, boosting shared prosperity, and feeding.

Farming's main potential contributions to rural development are supporting employment, ancillary businesses, and environmental services. Farming may be necessary in peripheral regions to support the economic and social infrastructure.

Rural development policies improve farming by improving on-farm activities and supporting ancillary services to secure sustainability.

Agriculture can help reduce poverty, raise incomes, and improve food security for most of the world's poor who live in rural areas and work mainly in farming. Enhancing agricultural productivity is essential for poverty reduction.

Agriculture also plays an integral part in rural development, primarily due to land use,

"One of the key elements of the Global Alliance is the Global Food and Nutrition Security Dashboard. Our goal is to pull timely and up-to-date information on the global food situation, development of the crisis, and the areas where action is needed in one place". Svenja Schulze (German Minister of Economic Cooperation and Development)

"At the World Bank, we recognise the importance of innovations and collaboration to promote food security. The Global Food and Nutrition Security Dashboard is an innovative knowledge platform that helps track food crises with real-time price monitoring and donor financing to get ahead of crises earlier and faster".Axel van Trotsenburg (World Bank Senior Managing Director)

About the Author

My life experience—from being an abandoned child eating from bins/gutters in Ghana to being one of the most successful businessmen in Europe— motivates me to write this book.

I used to follow my paternal grandmother to cocoa and other vegetable Farms in Ghana,

She was and is the best woman on earth who cared for me very well

I have visited most European countries and wish to share my experiences with my readers. I have also written over one hundred forty books and have many qualifications listed at the end of this book.

I have about six degrees, four post-graduates, including " institutional management, ten diplomas, 15 certificates, ect.

All are listed in this book.

Table of Contents

CHAPTER 1:   15

SUSTAINABLE AGRICULTURE FOR RURAL
DEVELOPMENT   15

1.Definition and Principles Sustainable Agriculture 15

2.Importance of Sustainability in Rural Development. 19

3Traditional vs. Modern Sustainable Practices   22

Traditional Sustainable Practices.   22

Modern Sustainable Practices.   25

Key Elements of Sustainable Agriculture. 28

1.Soil Health and Conservation.   28

1.1Importance of Soil Health.   29

1.2Practices for Soil Conservation.   29

CHAPTER 2:   32

WATER MANAGEMENT AND IRRIGATION
TECHNIQUES.   32

Importance of Sustainable Water Use   32

Sustainable Irrigation Techniques.   33

Crop Diversification and Rotation.   35

Importance of Crop Diversification   35

Benefits of Crop Rotation.   35

Diversified Cropping Systems   36

Organic Farming and Use of Natural Fertilizers. 38

Benefits of Organic Farming   38

Natural Fertilizer Options.   39

CHAPTER 3:   42

AGRO-ECOLOGICAL PRACTICES FOR RURAL
DEVELOPMENT.   42

Agroforestry and Its Role in Soil Conservation.   42

Benefits of Agroforestry for Soil Conservation.   43

Agroforestry Systems in Practice   44

Integrated Pest Management (IPM) Practices   46

Core Components of IPM.   46

Benefits of IPM for Rural Development   48

Examples of IPM in Action   48

Conservation Tillage and Its Benefits   49

Benefits of Conservation Tillage   50

Conservation Tillage Techniques   50

Crop-Livestock Integration Systems   51

Benefits of Crop-Livestock Integration   52

Examples of Crop-Livestock Integration   53

CHAPTER 4:   55

TECHNOLOGICAL INNOVATIONS IN SUSTAINABLE
AGRICULTURE.   55

Precision Agriculture for Resource Efficiency.   55

Critical Components of Precision Agriculture   56

Benefits of Precision Agriculture.   58

Use of Drones, Sensors, and Data Analytics in Farming.
60

Drones in Agriculture   60

Sensors in Agriculture   62

Data Analytics in Farming   62

Benefits of Drones, Sensors, and Data Analytics. 63

Mobile Applications for Rural Farmers   64

Types of Mobile Applications for Agriculture 65

Benefits of Mobile Applications for Rural Farmers. 66

Mobile Apps in Practice   68

Role of Biotechnology in Developing Resilient Crop
Varieties   68

Critical Biotechnology Applications in Agriculture. 69

Environmental of Biotechnology in Agriculture   70

Reduction in Pesticide Use.   71

Economic Impacts of Biotechnology.   72

Social Impacts of Biotechnology in Agriculture   74

Future Directions of Technological Innovations in
Sustainable Agriculture   76

CHAPTER 5:   78

CLIMATE-SMART AGRICULTURE   78

Climate Change Impacts on Rural Agriculture   78

Adaptation Strategies for Smallholder Farmers   82

Mitigation Practices, Such as Carbon Sequestration 86

Examples of Climate-Resilient Agricultural Systems 89

CHAPTER 6:   91

ECONOMIC VIABILITY SUSTAINABLE   91

1. Cost-Benefit Analysis of Sustainable vs. Conventional
Farming   92

2. Market Access and Value Chain Development for
Rural Farmers   95

3. Case Studies on Profitable Sustainable Farms 98

4. Role of Cooperatives and Farmer Associations 101

5.Future research areas   103

10

CHAPTER 7:   106

SOCIAL AND CULTURAL DIMENSIONS OF
SUSTAINABLE AGRICULTURE 106

1. Community-Based Approaches and Stakeholder
Engagement   106

2. Gender Roles in Sustainable Agriculture 110

3. Traditional Knowledge and Indigenous Practices 113

4. Youth Involvement and Succession Planning in
Farming   116

CHAPTER 8:   118

POLICIES AND GOVERNANCE FOR SUSTAINABLE
RURAL AGRICULTURE   118

1. Policies Supporting Sustainable Agriculture 119

2. Governments, NGOs, and International Bodies 121

3. Regulatory Frameworks for Organic and Sustainable
Products   125

4. Public-Private Partnerships in Promoting Rural
Development   128

CHAPTER 9:   131

CASE STUDIES OF SUCCESSFUL SUSTAINABLE
AGRICULTURE PROJECTS   131

1. India – Zero Budget Natural Farming (ZBNF) 131

Key Features of ZBNF -   131

Lessons Learned -   132

Factors Contributing to Success -   133

2.Brazil – Agroforestry Systems in the Amazon 134

Overview of the Project –   134

Key Features of Agroforestry Systems - 134

Lessons Learned -   135

Factors Contributing to Success -   136

Kenya – The Greenbelt Movement.   137

Overview of the Project –   137

Key Features of the Greenbelt Movement - 138

Lessons Learned -   138

Factors Contributing to Success -   139

3.Australia – The Land Care Movement.   141

Overview of the Project –   141

Key Features of Land Care -   141

Lessons Learned -   142

Factors Contributing to Success -   143

4.The Sustainable Agriculture Research Education
(SARE) Program   144

Overview of the Project –   144

Key Features of SARE -   144

Lessons Learned -   145

Factors Contributing to Success -   146

CHAPTER 10:   147

FUTURE DIRECTIONS FOR SUSTAINABLE
AGRICULTURE IN RURAL DEVELOPMENT 147

1. Emerging Trends and Technologies   147

2. Scaling Up Successful Models   152

3. Potential Areas for Research and Innovation 155

4. Sustainable Agriculture and Rural Resilience   157

CHAPTER 11:   160

GLOBAL AND REGIONAL POLICY FRAMEWORKS
FOR SUSTAINABLE DEVELOPMENT   160

International agreements and frameworks. 160

1. United Nations (UN) and Sustainable Development Goals (SDGs)   160

2. The World Trade Organization (WTO)   163

3. FAO's Role International Governance of Agriculture 164

4. Convention on Biological Diversity (CBD)   165

Regional Cooperation and Collaboration   166

1. African Union (AU) and the Comprehensive Africa Agriculture Development Programme (CAADP) 166

2. ASEAN (Association of Southeast Asian Nations) ASEAN Integrated Food Security Framework 167

3. Latin American and the Caribbean: The Agricultural Council of the Americas (CAA)   168

4. European Union (EU) and the Common Agricultural Policy (CAP)   169

5. The Pacific Islands: Pacific Islands Forum (PIF) 170

CHAPTER 12:   172

EDUCATION AND CAPACITY BUILDING IN RURAL AREAS   172

1. Building Human Capital in Rural Communities 172

A. Role of Education in Agricultural Development 173

B. Technical Training Farmer Extension Services 175

C. Farmer Education through Knowledge Sharing Platforms   176

2. Adult Learning and Extension Models   177

A. Non-Formal Education Models for Rural Farmers 177

B. Farmer-to-Farmer Extension   178

C. Community Engagement and Empowerment 179

3. Technology Literacy for Farmers   180

A. Importance of Digital Literacy in Agriculture 180

B. Access to Information and Market Integration 181

C. Bridging the Digital Divide   182

CHAPTER 13:   184

RURAL INFRASTRUCTURE FOR SUSTAINABLE
DEVELOPMENT   184

1. Transportation and Logistics   184

A. Improving Rural Transport Networks   185

B. Efficient Logistics Supply Chain Management 186

2. Post-Harvest Technology and Storage   187

A. Post-Harvest Losses   188

B. Innovative Solutions for Preserving and Storing
Produce   189

3. Access to Renewable Energy   191

A. Solar Energy for Rural Farming Communities   191

B. Wind Energy for Rural Areas   193

C. Biogas for Rural Farming   194

References   203

CHAPTER 1:

SUSTAINABLE AGRICULTURE FOR RURAL DEVELOPMENT

Sustainable agriculture is a method of farming that meets the current food needs without compromising the ability of future generations to meet theirs. This approach prioritises environmental health, economic profitability, and social and economic equity, focusing on long-term viability over immediate gains.

1. Definition and Principles of Sustainable Agriculture

Sustainable agriculture is an agricultural system that emphasises preserving and enhancing natural resources, reducing environmental impacts, and supporting farming communities' social and economic welfare. This concept emerged as a response to concerns about industrial agriculture's ecological degradation and aimed to integrate farming into the natural ecosystem sustainably.

Principles of Sustainable Agriculture:

Environmental Health:

Sustainable agriculture seeks to maintain and improve the natural environment. Practices involve reducing dependency on chemical inputs like pesticides and synthetic fertilisers, conserving water, supporting soil health, and fostering biodiversity. Healthier ecosystems also enhance pest control, pollination, and climate resilience.

1. Economic Viability:

A core aspect of sustainable agriculture is ensuring that farming practices are economically viable in the long term. This means creating agricultural systems that produce sufficient yields and support fair wages, reducing input costs, and enhancing productivity through natural and cost-effective means.

2. Social and Economic Equity:

Sustainable agriculture recognises the role of farmers and rural communities in the food system, supporting fair treatment, wages, and working conditions. It also ensures that rural development benefits local communities and promotes gender equality, fair labour practices, and resource access.

3. Biodiversity Conservation:

Sustainable agriculture strengthens resilience to pests, diseases, and climatic variations by conserving biodiversity. Crop rotation, agroforestry, and integrated pest management (IPM) are examples of biodiversity-oriented practices that foster balance within the ecosystem and reduce the reliance on chemical inputs.

4. Resource Efficiency and Waste Reduction:

Sustainable agricultural practices, such as efficiently using water, soil, and energy, maximise resource efficiency. Techniques like composting, recycling agrarian waste, and employing renewable energy sources help reduce farming's environmental footprint.

5. Adaptability and Innovation:

Sustainable agriculture requires continuous adaptation to changing environmental, economic, and social conditions. Farmers are encouraged to innovate by integrating modern technology with traditional practices, seeking climate-smart approaches, and adopting new, more sustainable methods as they become available.

2. Importance of Sustainability in Rural Development.

Rural areas typically have agriculture as the backbone of the economy, and sustainable agriculture plays a pivotal role in these regions' economic stability, food security, and environmental health. Sustainable agriculture contributes to rural development in several critical ways:

1. Food Security and Nutrition:

Sustainable agricultural practices enhance food availability, dietary diversity, and nutrition outcomes. Rural communities that rely on local production for food can benefit from year-round access to safe and nutritious foods, mitigating malnutrition and hunger.

2. Economic Growth and Employment:

Sustainable farming can make agriculture more resilient and profitable, creating stable and well-paying jobs in rural areas and reducing poverty.

Since rural communities often depend on agriculture, improved productivity and economic security from sustainable practices support rural development.

3. Environmental Conservation:

Traditional and industrial farming methods have led to soil degradation, water pollution, and biodiversity loss, disproportionately affecting rural communities. Sustainable practices help restore natural resources and reduce environmental degradation, which is vital for the long-term prosperity of rural communities.

4. Empowerment of Small Farmers:

Sustainable agriculture often involves diversified production and local markets, allowing small-scale farmers to retain a more significant share of their profits. Sustainable practices empower farmers by focusing on value-added products and encouraging direct access to markets, giving them greater control over their livelihoods.

5. Resilience to Climate Change:

Rural areas, especially those in developing countries, are often more vulnerable to climate change. Sustainable practices—crop diversification, agroforestry, and conservation agriculture—build resilience to climate shocks like droughts, floods, and extreme temperatures.

6. Social Cohesion and Community Engagement: Sustainable agriculture promotes community-based models where rural farmers collaborate, share knowledge, and work together to overcome shared challenges. It creates social bonds, strengthens community structures, and enhances rural communities' ability to manage resources.

3. Traditional vs. Modern Sustainable Practices

The history of sustainable agriculture is rooted in traditional farming practices that emphasise harmony with the natural environment. However, modern sustainable agriculture has incorporated scientific advancements and technological innovation, combining traditional methods' wisdom with contemporary approaches' efficiency.

Traditional Sustainable Practices.

Traditional agriculture methods often align with sustainable principles due to their natural alignment with ecological cycles. Here are some critical conventional practices that contribute to sustainability:

1. Crop Rotation and Polyculture:

For centuries, farmers rotated crops and grew multiple crops in the same field to maintain soil health and prevent pest build-up. Polyculture,

22

growing diverse crops together, reduces the risk of pest outbreaks and improves soil fertility without chemical inputs.

2. Agroforestry:

Agroforestry, the practice of growing trees alongside crops, provides multiple benefits, like improving soil structure, preventing erosion, and supporting biodiversity. Trees serve as windbreaks, provide shade, and offer habitats for various species.

3. Use of Organic Fertilizers:

Traditional farming methods relied on organic fertilisers, such as manure and compost, to replenish soil nutrients. These natural inputs enrich the soil, improve its structure, and reduce dependency on synthetic fertilisers.

4. Water Conservation Techniques:

Indigenous farming communities developed methods to conserve water, including terracing, canal systems, and rainwater harvesting. These methods minimised water use and protected local water resources, promoting long-term agricultural productivity.

5. Local Seeds and Genetic Diversity:

Traditional farmers often save seeds yearly, promoting genetic diversity in crops and making them more resilient to diseases, pests, and climate change. This practice also allowed communities to adapt crops to local conditions.

Modern Sustainable Practices.

Modern sustainable agriculture has introduced new techniques that build upon and enhance traditional practices. These practices leverage scientific research, technology, and innovation to create more efficient, resilient, and productive farming systems.

1. Integrated Pest Management (IPM):

IPM is a strategy that combines biological, cultural, physical, and chemical tools to manage pests with minimal environmental impact. It emphasises biological control methods, like introducing natural predators, to reduce reliance on chemical pesticides.

2. Precision Agriculture:

Precision agriculture uses technology, such as GPS, drones, and sensors, to apply inputs like water, fertilisers, and pesticides only where and when needed. This approach reduces waste, minimises environmental impact, and increases crop yields.

3. Conservation Tillage:

Conservation tillage practices, like no-till and low-till farming, reduce soil disturbance and preserve soil structure. These practices reduce erosion, increase water infiltration, and support soil biodiversity, creating healthier soils and more resilient crops.

4. Soil Health Management:

Modern sustainable practices prioritise soil health through cover cropping, crop rotations, and organic amendments. These methods help maintain soil fertility, prevent erosion, and improve water retention, essential for long-term productivity.

5. Renewable Energy in Agriculture:

Integrating renewable energy sources, such as solar panels, wind turbines, and bioenergy systems, into farming operations reduces dependence on fossil fuels. By using renewable energy, farms can lower greenhouse gas emissions and reduce operational costs.

6. Vertical Farming and Hydroponics:

These innovative methods of growing crops in controlled environments require less land and water than traditional field farming. Vertical farming, particularly in urban areas, and hydroponics reduce resource use while producing high-quality yields year-round.

7. Agro-ecology and Permaculture:

Agroecology and permaculture draw from traditional methods but apply scientific principles to design highly sustainable agricultural systems. These practices emphasise diversity, resilience, and ecosystem functionality, aiming to create closed-loop, self-sustaining systems.

Key Elements of Sustainable Agriculture.

Sustainable agriculture is essential for maintaining food security, enhancing ecosystem health, and supporting rural communities. It integrates practices that reduce environmental impacts and promote long-term agricultural productivity. The four critical elements outlined below—soil health and conservation, water management and irrigation, crop diversification and rotation, and organic farming—are essential to achieving a balanced and sustainable agricultural system.

1. Soil Health and Conservation.

Healthy soil is the foundation of sustainable agriculture. Soil supports crop growth by providing essential nutrients, water, and a structure for root systems. It also plays a significant role in carbon sequestration and mitigating the impacts of climate change. However, intensive agricultural practices, such as monoculture and excessive tilling, degrade soil health, leading to erosion, nutrient depletion, and reduced fertility.

1.1 Importance of Soil Health.

Soil health is directly related to organic matter, nutrient availability, and biodiversity within the soil ecosystem. Microbial organisms, earthworms, and fungi contribute to soil structure and fertility, naturally enhancing crop productivity (Lal, 2020).

Sustainable agriculture practices can improve crop resilience against pests, diseases, and environmental stressors by maintaining healthy soil.

1.2 Practices for Soil Conservation.

1. Cover Cropping:

Cover crops, such as legumes and grasses, are planted during off-seasons to protect soil from erosion, suppress weeds, and enrich soil organic matter. Cover crops can also fix nitrogen in the soil, reducing the need for synthetic fertilisers (Tilman et al., 2011).

2. Reduced Tillage:

Conservation tillage practices, including no-till and reduced-till farming, help maintain soil structure and organic matter. By leaving crop residues on the field these practices prevent soil compaction, improve water infiltration, and reduce erosion (Holland, 2004).

3. Composting and Organic Amendments:
 Adding compost or organic matter to soil helps increase its fertility, water retention, and structure. Compost enriches soil biodiversity and supplies essential nutrients, which improves plant growth and reduces the need for chemical fertilisers (Tautges et al., 2019).

4. Agroforestry and Tree Planting:

Integrating trees and shrubs within agricultural land can prevent soil erosion, improve water retention, and increase biodiversity. Tree roots stabilise soil, reduce surface runoff, and create a favourable microclimate for crops (Nair, 1993).

5. Contour Farming and Terracing:

These techniques prevent soil erosion in hilly areas. Contour farming involves ploughing along the contours of the land, while terracing creates stepped levels on slopes. Both reduce water runoff and soil loss (Pimentel, 2006).

CHAPTER 2:

WATER MANAGEMENT AND IRRIGATION TECHNIQUES.

Water is a precious resource in agriculture, and sustainable water management practices ensure the efficient use, conservation, and protection of water resources. Effective water management is especially critical in regions where water scarcity threatens food production.

Importance of Sustainable Water Use

Agriculture accounts for nearly 70% of global freshwater use, and inefficient irrigation practices can lead to water wastage and soil salinisation (FAO, 2017).

Sustainable water management can help conserve water resources, increase crop yields, and reduce the environmental impact of farming practices.

Sustainable Irrigation Techniques.

Drip Irrigation:

Drip irrigation delivers water directly to the plant roots through tubes and emitters, reducing water wastage and evaporation losses. It is particularly effective in arid regions with limited water resources (Yuan et al., 2015).

Rainwater Harvesting:

Collecting and storing rainwater allows farmers to use it during dry periods, reducing dependence on external water sources. Rainwater harvesting can be as simple as using barrels to collect rain or constructing ponds to capture larger quantities (Rockström et al., 2002).

Mulching:

Mulching involves covering soil with organic or inorganic materials like straw, leaves, or plastic. Mulch reduces water evaporation, controls weeds, and maintains soil temperature, which reduces the need for irrigation (Li et al., 2020).

Soil Moisture Management:

Monitoring soil moisture levels using sensors can help farmers apply water only when needed, reducing over-irrigation and conserving water resources. Moisture sensors can be combined with other precision agriculture tools for optimal water use (Zhang et al., 2019).

Alternative Water Sources:

Sustainable agriculture promotes using non-traditional water sources, like treated wastewater, for irrigation in regions with water scarcity. This practice conserves freshwater resources while safely providing water for crops (Qadir et al., 2010).

Crop Diversification and Rotation.

Crop diversification and rotation are essential for maintaining soil health, reducing pest pressure, and enhancing resilience against environmental stresses. These practices prevent the adverse effects of monoculture and contribute to long-term productivity.

Importance of Crop Diversification

Crop diversification improves ecosystem resilience, reduces market risks, and enhances farm biodiversity (Pretty, 2008).

By diversifying crops, farmers can reduce their dependency on a single crop, stabilise income, and improve food security.

Benefits of Crop Rotation.

Crop rotation, or changing crop types of each season, prevents the build-up of pests and diseases associated with monoculture, as different crops have different pest and nutrient needs (Liebman & Dyck, 1993).

For example, rotating legumes with cereal crops replenishes soil nitrogen because legumes naturally fix nitrogen in the soil, enhancing the fertility of subsequent crops (Snapp et al., 2010).

Diversified Cropping Systems

Intercropping:

Growing multiple crops in the same field increases biodiversity and optimises space. By allowing plants to complement each other's nutrient needs, intercropping can reduce pest problems and improve yields (Lithourgidis et al., 2011).

Agroforestry Systems:

Agroforestry integrates trees with crops or livestock, creating a diverse system that provides multiple products and ecosystem services, such as wind protection and soil enrichment (Garrity, 2004).

Sequential Cropping:

This technique involves planting two or more crops in the same field within a single growing season. Maintaining soil cover year-round maximises land use, reduces erosion, and improves crop productivity (Kassam et al., 2020).

Cover Cropping:

During the off-season, planting cover crops, like clover or rye, improves soil health, prevents erosion, and prepares the land for the next crop cycle (Weil & Brady, 2016).

Polyculture Systems:

Polyculture is a form of crop diversification where farmers grow multiple crop species in the same field. It mimics natural ecosystems, increases biodiversity, and reduces vulnerability to pest outbreaks (Lin, 2011).

Organic Farming and Use of Natural Fertilizers.

Organic farming avoids synthetic chemicals, relying instead on natural processes to fertilise soil, manage pests, and promote crop growth. Organic practices are integral to sustainable agriculture because they reduce environmental impacts and support ecosystem health.

Benefits of Organic Farming

Organic farming promotes soil fertility, conserves biodiversity, and supports natural pest management. Organic methods improve soil structure, increase organic matter, and enhance water retention, which benefits plant health and yield (Reganold & Wachter, 2016).

Organic products also meet consumer demand for food grown without synthetic chemicals, contributing to sustainable farms' market value and economic viability.

Natural Fertilizer Options.

Compost and Manure:

Composting organic matter, such as crop residues and animal manure, creates a nutrient-rich soil amendment. Compost improves soil structure, fertility, and microbial activity, promoting healthy crop growth (Edwards et al., 2004).

Green Manure:

Green manure crops, such as legumes, are grown specifically to be ploughed back into the soil, providing nutrients and organic matter. Green manures enrich soil with nitrogen, enhance biodiversity, and suppress weeds (Snapp et al., 2005).

Biofertilizers:

Biofertilisers contain beneficial microbes that enhance plant nutrient availability. For instance, rhizobium bacteria in legume crops fix atmospheric nitrogen, providing a natural nitrogen source for plants (Bashan et al., 2014).

Fish Emulsion and Seaweed Extracts:

These natural fertilisers are rich in nutrients and support plant growth by providing a slow-release source of essential minerals. Fish emulsion is nitrogenous, while seaweed extracts provide micronutrients, growth hormones, and stress tolerance (Khan et al., 2009).

Rock Phosphate and Lime:

Natural mineral sources, such as rock phosphate and lime, supply essential nutrients, such as phosphorus and calcium, which are crucial for plant development. These amendments help adjust soil pH and enhance nutrient availability (Roy et al., 2006).

Integrated Pest Management (IPM):

Organic farming often includes IPM strategies, which rely on natural predators, beneficial insects, and crop diversity to control pest populations. This approach minimises chemical pesticides and reduces environmental contamination (Lewis et al., 1997).

CHAPTER 3:

AGRO-ECOLOGICAL PRACTICES FOR RURAL
DEVELOPMENT.

Agroecology is a holistic approach that combines ecological principles with agricultural practices to create sustainable and resilient farming systems. This approach emphasises biodiversity, resource conservation, and the integration of local knowledge to support rural development. The agroecological practices discussed here—agroforestry, integrated pest management, conservation tillage, and crop-livestock integration—are essential for achieving these goals, particularly in rural areas where natural resources are vital for livelihoods.

Agroforestry and Its Role in Soil Conservation.

Agroforestry integrates trees and shrubs with crops and livestock systems to create a diverse, sustainable agricultural landscape. It offers numerous environmental, economic, and social benefits that contribute to rural development, especially in areas with degraded soils.

42

Benefits of Agroforestry for Soil Conservation.

Erosion Control:

Tree and shrub roots help anchor the soil, reducing erosion caused by wind and water. This is especially beneficial in hilly and mountainous rural areas, where erosion can severely impact arable land (Nair, 1993).

Nutrient Cycling:

Trees in agroforestry systems help recycle nutrients from deep soil layers, bringing them to the surface through leaf litter and root decay. It replenishes soil fertility and reduces the need for chemical fertilisers, which can be costly for rural farmers (Jose, 2009).

Enhanced Soil Structure and Organic Matter:

Adding organic matter from decomposing leaves and roots improves soil structure, water retention, and microbial diversity. It enhances soil health and productivity over the long term (Lal, 2004).

Agroforestry Systems in Practice

Alley Cropping:

In alley cropping, crops are grown between rows of trees or shrubs. This method protects crops from solid winds, reduces water evaporation, and creates a microclimate that can improve yields (Garrett et al., 2009).

Silvopasture:

This system combines forestry with livestock grazing, where animals graze beneath trees. Silvopasture increases income opportunities and provides shelter for livestock, while the trees contribute to soil conservation and water cycle regulation (Sharrow, 2007).

Windbreaks and Shelterbelts:

Trees planted as windbreaks prevent soil erosion by reducing wind speed. This technique is particularly effective in protecting crops, reducing soil moisture loss, and enhancing habitat diversity on rural farms (Kort, 1988).

Integrated Pest Management (IPM) Practices

Integrated Pest Management (IPM) is a strategic approach to pest control that uses biological, cultural, physical, and chemical methods to manage pests sustainably. IPM reduces reliance on chemical pesticides, benefiting the environment and rural farming communities.

Core Components of IPM.

Biological Control:

This involves introducing natural predators, parasites, or pathogens to control pest populations. For example, ladybugs can help control aphid populations, while parasitic wasps target caterpillars. Biological control minimises the need for chemical interventions (Kogan, 1998).

Cultural Control:

Adjusting farming practices, such as crop rotation, planting pest-resistant crop varieties, and using intercropping techniques, can prevent pest

46

infestations. These methods disrupt pest breeding cycles and reduce crop pressure (Lewis et al., 1997).

Physical and Mechanical Control:

Techniques such as trapping, manual removal, and physical barriers prevent pest access to crops. For example, row covers can protect crops from insect pests without chemicals (Pedigo & Rice, 2009).

Benefits of IPM for Rural Development

Cost-Effectiveness:
Reducing reliance on chemical pesticides saves farmers money, which is especially important for small-scale rural farmers with limited financial resources (Parsa et al., 2014).

Reduced Environmental Impact:
By limiting pesticide use, IPM protects beneficial insects, preserves soil health, and reduces water contamination, which supports biodiversity and ecosystem services vital to agriculture (FAO, 2017).

Improved Crop Resilience:
IPM encourages diversification of pest control methods, which makes crops more resilient to pests and less vulnerable to pest outbreaks (Pretty, 2008).

Examples of IPM in Action

Trap Cropping:

Planting certain crops that attract pests away from the main crop reduces damage to the primary crop. For example, planting mustard around tomatoes can attract pests away from the main crop (Shelton & Badenes-Perez, 2006).

Push-Pull Technology:

In maize farming, "push" crops like Desmodium repel pests, while "pull" crops like Napier grass attract them. This strategy has effectively controlled sub-Saharan Africa's pests like the stem borer (Khan et al., 2008).

Conservation Tillage and Its Benefits

Conservation tillage minimises soil disturbance, helping to maintain soil structure, reduce erosion, and increase water retention. By keeping crop residues on the soil surface, conservation tillage supports biodiversity and enhances soil fertility, which benefits rural farmers in the long term.

Benefits of Conservation Tillage

Reduced Soil Erosion:

Leaving crop residues on the soil surface protects against wind and water erosion. It is particularly important in rural areas where soil loss can threaten agricultural productivity and local food security (Derpsch et al., 2010).

Increased Soil Organic Matter:
Conservation tillage allows organic matter from plant residues to decompose slowly, enhancing soil fertility and microbial activity over time (Lal, 2004).

Improved Water Retention:
Conservation tillage helps soil retain water by reducing evaporation and increasing soil porosity, vital for crops in arid and semi-arid regions (Hobbs, 2007).

Conservation Tillage Techniques

No-Till Farming:

Seeds are directly sown into undisturbed soil in no-till systems. This method conserves soil moisture and reduces erosion, making it suitable for drought-prone areas (Kassam et al., 2020).

Strip Tillage:

This technique tills only the rows where seeds will be planted, leaving the rest of the field undisturbed. It conserves soil moisture and organic matter, promoting a healthier ecosystem (Blevins & Frye, 1993).

Mulching:

Covering soil with organic or inorganic mulch reduces evaporation, suppresses weeds, and regulates soil temperature. Mulching mainly benefits small-scale rural farmers by reducing irrigation needs and labour costs (Teasdale, 2007).

Crop-Livestock Integration Systems

Crop-livestock integration combines crop production and livestock rearing within a single farming system. This method creates a closed-loop system that maximises resource use, enhances soil fertility, and provides multiple sources of income, all crucial for rural development.

Benefits of Crop-Livestock Integration

Nutrient Recycling:

Livestock manure enriches soil with organic matter and essential nutrients, reducing the need for synthetic fertilisers. This nutrient recycling improves soil health and crop yields (Russell et al., 2007).

Diversified Income Sources:

Farmers can generate income from multiple sources by integrating crops and livestock, reducing financial risks, and enhancing food security for rural communities (Herrero et al., 2010).

Increased Resilience:

Crop-livestock systems are more resilient to market fluctuations and climate impacts. Livestock provides a fallback resource during crop failures and can help farmers recover from losses (Dixon et al., 2001).

Examples of Crop-Livestock Integration

Manure Application for Soil Fertility:

Livestock manure fertilises fields, providing a natural, cost-effective nutrient source that improves soil structure and promotes crop growth (Powell et al., 2004).

Grazing Cover Crops:

Livestock can graze on cover crops planted after the main harvest, reducing the need for forage production and providing animals with a nutritious food source. This practice also recycles nutrients into the soil (Franzluebbers, 2007).

Dual-Purpose Crops:

Some crops, like maize, can be grown for grain and fodder, supporting livestock feed while providing a primary harvest for human consumption. This approach maximises land use efficiency in rural areas (Seré & Steinfeld, 1996).

CHAPTER 4:

TECHNOLOGICAL INNOVATIONS IN
SUSTAINABLE AGRICULTURE.

Sustainable agriculture has grown increasingly critical in today's world, especially as agricultural systems strive to meet the demands of a growing population, combat climate change, and conserve natural resources. With the help of technological advancements, farmers now have tools to improve productivity while maintaining ecological balance. Four main technological innovations are pivotal in this transformation: precision agriculture, drones and sensors, mobile applications tailored for rural farmers, and biotechnology's impact on crop resilience. Below is a comprehensive exploration of these technologies and how they contribute to sustainability in agriculture.

Precision Agriculture for Resource Efficiency.

Precision agriculture is an innovative farming management concept that leverages technology to optimise resource use, improve crop yield, and reduce ecological footprint. It relies on data-driven techniques to help farmers make better decisions about resource application across different field sections, minimising waste and promoting sustainability.

Critical Components of Precision Agriculture

Global Positioning System (GPS) and Geographic Information System (GIS) Technology

Precision agriculture relies heavily on GPS and GIS technologies, allowing farmers to create accurate field maps and monitor spatial variations in soil properties, crop health, and pest infestations. Through GPS, farm equipment can be guided with precision, allowing for tasks like seeding, spraying, and harvesting to be conducted with extreme accuracy. GIS complements this by layering spatial data, helping farmers manage variations within a field to optimise input use (Swinton et al., 2015).

Variable Rate Technology (VRT)

VRT empowers farmers to adjust the application of inputs, such as fertilisers, water, and pesticides, according to the needs of specific areas within a field. With VRT, inputs are applied precisely where needed, reducing waste, lowering input costs, and minimising the environmental impact. It also helps prevent over-application, leading to nutrient runoff and pollution (Robert, 2002).

Yield Monitoring Systems

These systems are installed on harvesting equipment to measure crop yield in real time. By recording the yield data, farmers can evaluate which areas of a field produce more or less crops. This insight helps identify areas needing more nutrients, better water management, or pest control interventions. Yield monitoring systems are crucial for improving crop management and achieving higher, more sustainable yields over time (Cook & Bramley, 1998).

Benefits of Precision Agriculture.

Efficient Resource Utilization.

Precision agriculture allows farmers to apply water, fertilisers, and pesticides only where necessary, conserving resources and reducing operational costs. For instance, using VRT to apply water or fertiliser based on soil moisture levels or nutrient needs enhances yield and efficiency.

Improved Crop Yields

By tailoring practices to specific areas within a field, farmers can achieve more consistent and healthier crop growth, leading to higher yields. The precise application of inputs maximises the productive capacity of each field section, benefiting farmers financially and ecologically.

Reduced Environmental Impact

Precision agriculture helps prevent problems associated with traditional farming methods, such as fertiliser runoff, which can lead to water pollution.

Using GPS and VRT, farmers minimise the amount of chemical runoff, decreasing the environmental impact and supporting cleaner ecosystems.

Use of Drones, Sensors, and Data Analytics in Farming.

Drones, sensors, and data analytics provide farmers with real-time insights into crop health, soil conditions, and weather patterns. By combining aerial imaging, on-ground sensors, and data analytics, farmers can make proactive decisions to ensure optimal crop growth and minimise loss due to environmental changes.

Drones in Agriculture

Aerial Imaging and Mapping.

Drones with cameras and sensors can capture high-resolution images of entire fields. Farmers can detect crop stress, nutrient deficiencies, pest infestations, and water issues by examining these images. Drone imaging provides a bird' s-eye view of a field, highlighting areas that need attention and allowing farmers to address problems before they become widespread (Zhang & Kovacs, 2012).

Crop Health Monitoring.

Drones with multispectral or thermal sensors can measure crop health by detecting stress indicators, such as chlorophyll levels and plant temperature variations. By identifying these signs early, farmers can promptly apply necessary interventions, such as irrigation or pest control (Nebiker et al., 2008).

Sensors in Agriculture

Soil Moisture Sensors

Soil moisture sensors are placed in the soil to measure water content at different depths. By providing real-time soil moisture data, these sensors help farmers determine the optimal time and amount of irrigation needed, preventing overwatering and conserving water resources. They are especially useful in areas prone to drought or water scarcity (Jones, 2004).

Nutrient Sensors

Nutrient sensors measure soil nutrient levels, helping farmers apply fertilisers more accurately. This technology prevents nutrient overload, which can lead to leaching and pollution of water bodies. By ensuring that fertilisers are used only where necessary, nutrient sensors help maintain soil health and ecosystem balance (Sudduth et al., 1997).

Data Analytics in Farming

Predictive Analytics for Crop Management.

Predictive analytics uses historical and real-time data to forecast crop performance and potential risks. For instance, predictive models can suggest the best time for planting or harvesting based on weather trends and soil conditions. This proactive approach helps minimise risks and maximise productivity, making farms more resilient to climate and market changes (McBratney et al., 2005).

Decision Support Systems (DSS).

DSS uses data analytics to provide farmers with actionable insights and recommendations on crop management, pest control, and resource use. DSS especially benefits smallholders, offering scientific advice to optimise farm operations and improve productivity (Antle et al., 2017).

Benefits of Drones, Sensors, and Data Analytics.

Enhanced Crop Monitoring

Real-time monitoring allows farmers to address problems quickly, improving crop health and yield. Drone and sensor data provide a clear picture of the field, helping farmers implement timely interventions.

Optimized Input Use

By assessing real-time data on soil, crop, and weather conditions, farmers can optimise their input use, reducing waste and environmental impact.

Proactive Decision-Making.

Data-driven insights enable farmers to anticipate pest outbreaks or nutrient deficiencies, allowing for proactive management and greater resilience.

Mobile Applications for Rural Farmers

Mobile applications

Mobile technology is a powerful tool for rural farmers. It provides valuable information on weather, market prices, farming techniques, and more. These apps empower farmers with the knowledge and resources they need to make informed decisions, increase productivity, and access markets.

Types of Mobile Applications for Agriculture

Weather Forecast Apps

Apps like Plantix or Agrible provide localised weather forecasts, helping farmers plan their activities around expected weather patterns. This is especially important for smallholders, who often depend on rainfall for irrigation. Knowing the weather in advance helps farmers avoid losses due to unexpected rain or drought (Davis et al., 2019).

Market Price Apps

Market price apps, such as Fisheries and Esoko, allow farmers to check the current prices for crops and livestock in nearby markets. This information empowers farmers to negotiate better prices and avoid intermediaries who may undercut their earnings.

Farm Management Apps

Apps like FarmLogs and AgriApp help farmers track expenses, manage resources, and monitor crop health. By keeping records and monitoring farm operations, these apps help farmers make better management decisions, improving overall productivity.

Benefits of Mobile Applications for Rural Farmers.

Access to Real-Time Information

Mobile apps provide instant updates on weather, crop health, and market prices, enabling farmers to make informed decisions that reduce risks and maximise returns.

Increased Market Connectivity

Apps that offer market price information help farmers avoid intermediaries, enabling them to sell directly and secure fairer prices.

Enhanced Knowledge and Training

Many apps provide farming tips, tutorials, and best practices, allowing farmers to adopt new techniques and improve their skills, contributing to higher productivity and better yields.

Mobile Apps in Practice

iCow (Kenya)

iCow is an app that offers advice on cattle breeding, feeding schedules, disease prevention, and improving dairy productivity to Kenyan dairy farmers.

Kisan Suvidha (India)

This app offers Indian farmers weather forecasts, market prices, and best practices for crop management, empowering rural farmers with the knowledge to improve yields and profitability.

Role of Biotechnology in Developing Resilient Crop Varieties

Biotechnology in agriculture involves genetic modification, molecular markers, and gene editing techniques to create crop varieties resilient to pests, diseases, and environmental stresses. Biotechnology enhances food security by enabling the production of crops that can withstand adverse conditions, ensuring sustainable production even as climate challenges increase.

Critical Biotechnology Applications in Agriculture.

Genetically Modified (GM)

Crops are engineered to express desirable traits, such as resistance to pests or tolerance to herbicides. For example, BT cotton has been modified to produce a natural pesticide, reducing the need for chemical pesticides and making cotton farming more sustainable (James, 2015).

Marker-Assisted Selection (MAS)

MAS uses molecular markers to identify desirable genetic traits in crops. It accelerates breeding programs, allowing scientists to develop varieties with traits like disease resistance or drought tolerance without directly modifying genes (Collard & Mackill, 2008).

Gene Editing (CRISPR)

CRISPR technology allows precise editing of specific genes, enabling scientists to improve crop characteristics more accurately. For example, CRISPR can be used to develop rice varieties that can survive flooding, a valuable trait as climate change leads to more extreme weather events (Wang et al., 2014).

Environmental Impacts of Biotechnology in Agriculture.

Reduction in Pesticide Use.

One of the prominent environmental benefits of biotechnology, particularly with genetically modified (GM) crops like Bt (Bacillus thuringiensis) varieties, is reducing the need for chemical pesticides. Crops engineered to resist pests inherently minimise pesticide usage, minimise chemical runoff into soil and water bodies and contribute to healthier ecosystems. This reduced pesticide need also limits harm to beneficial insects, such as pollinators, essential for biodiversity and ecological balance (Shelton et al., 2002).

Soil Health Preservation.

Biotechnology can indirectly promote soil health by minimising the use of herbicides and pesticides, which are known to degrade soil quality over time. By using herbicide-tolerant crops, for example, farmers can reduce the amount of herbicide applied and more easily adopt conservation tillage practices. Conservation tillage helps retain soil structure and prevent erosion, leading to improved soil health and sustainability in the long run (Carpenter, 2011).

Drought and Flood Resilience

Biotechnology enables the development of crops with enhanced tolerance to drought and flooding. Crops such as drought-resistant maize and flood-tolerant rice help farmers in areas prone to these extreme conditions maintain productivity even when faced with environmental stressors. Using these crops contributes to resource efficiency by requiring less water and reducing the dependency on irrigation, which helps conserve water in drought-affected areas and reduces energy costs associated with irrigation systems (Rivera et al., 2016).

Economic Impacts of Biotechnology.

· Increased Crop Yields and Productivity.

Biotechnology allows farmers to cultivate high-yielding varieties with traits that enhance productivity. For example, disease-resistant varieties are more likely to reach maturity, thus increasing overall crop yield. Higher yields mean farmers can produce more food on the same land, supporting food security and enabling economies to sustain their growing populations more effectively (Brookes & Barfoot, 2018).

· Cost Savings for Farmers

Biotechnology reduces operational costs by reducing the need for inputs like pesticides. For example, with Bt cotton, farmers save on the costs associated with chemical pest control, which translates to significant savings over time. Furthermore, crops more resilient to environmental stresses reduce the losses associated with failed harvests, providing economic stability to farmers and encouraging long-term agricultural investments (Huang et al., 2015).

· Enhanced Market Access for Farmers.

Biotechnology can significantly increase farmers' market access in developing regions by making them more competitive. High-quality, resilient crops

73

have a better chance of meeting market demands and can even attract premium prices in some cases. Biotechnology-enhanced crops, especially with certification for sustainability or organic farming, can open new market opportunities for rural farmers and increase their income potential (Fernandez-Cornejo et al., 2014).

Social Impacts of Biotechnology in Agriculture

· Enhanced Food Security

Biotechnology supports food security by ensuring a stable supply of crops resistant to environmental challenges, pests, and diseases. In regions prone to food shortages, biotechnology can be particularly beneficial by enabling farmers to produce sufficient food despite unpredictable climate conditions, thereby reducing dependency on food imports and enhancing community resilience (Qaim & Kouser, 2013).

· Empowerment of Smallholder Farmers.

Biotechnology can benefit farmers by providing crop varieties that require fewer inputs and produce higher yields. By increasing productivity and reducing dependency on costly chemicals, biotechnology enhances smallholders' profitability and helps them achieve a more sustainable livelihood. When smallholder farmers gain access to resilient crop varieties, they are empowered to participate more actively in the economy and improve their overall quality of life (Glover, 2010).

· Educational and Skill-Building Opportunities,

Integrating biotechnology into agriculture often comes with educational initiatives that train farmers in properly using and managing biotech crops. These initiatives enhance farmers' agricultural skills and help build their capacity to adopt other innovative farming practices. Such training programs are precious in rural areas, where educational opportunities can be limited, and they support the long-term development of agricultural communities (Anderson et al., 2005).

Future Directions of Technological Innovations in Sustainable Agriculture

Integrating technology into sustainable agriculture has opened up vast opportunities for improving efficiency, reducing environmental impact, and supporting the livelihoods of rural farmers. As we've explored, innovations like precision agriculture, drones and data analytics, mobile applications, and biotechnology contribute to a more sustainable and resilient agricultural sector.

While these technologies hold significant promise, it is also essential to consider some challenges and areas for further research and improvement:

Accessibility and Affordability

Smallholders and rural farmers still have limited access to advanced technology due to high costs and lacking infrastructure. Ensuring that these technologies are affordable and accessible to all farmers will be crucial to maximising their impact.

Education and Training.

Farmers must receive adequate training and support to implement technological innovations successfully. Programs that educate farmers about technology use, data interpretation, and sustainable practices will be essential for long-term success.

Policy and Investment Support.

Governments, organisations, and private investors can support adopting sustainable technologies through subsidies, grants, and favourable policies. Encouraging investment in agricultural technology research can accelerate the development of innovations suited to specific regional needs.

Environmental Considerations

Continued research is needed to evaluate the long-term environmental impacts of biotechnology and other technologies to ensure they contribute to sustainability without unintended ecological harm.

CHAPTER 5:

CLIMATE-SMART AGRICULTURE

Climate-smart agriculture (CSA) is an approach developed to address the challenges of food security and climate change. As climate change continues to alter weather patterns, disrupt ecosystems, and impact agricultural production, CSA aims to create resilient and sustainable systems. Below, we explore CSA's core aspects: the impact of climate change on rural agriculture, adaptation strategies for smallholder farmers, mitigation practices, and examples of climate-resilient agricultural systems. This guide is structured to give detailed, student-friendly explanations of each aspect.

Climate Change Impacts on Rural Agriculture

Climate change poses significant threats to agriculture, with impacts especially pronounced in rural areas where agricultural activities are often a primary livelihood. The adverse effects of climate change on agriculture arise from changes in temperature, precipitation, and the frequency and intensity of extreme weather events.

Rising Temperatures

In many regions, increased temperatures directly impact crop growth cycles. Crops have specific temperature ranges within which they thrive, and extreme heat can disrupt photosynthesis, reduce crop yields, and even cause crop failure. For instance, staple crops like maise, wheat, and rice are particularly vulnerable to heat stress, leading to lower productivity. Increased temperatures can also exacerbate pest and disease infestations, further threatening crop yields (IPCC, 2014).

Altered Rainfall Patterns

Changing precipitation patterns affect water availability, which is crucial for crop growth. In some areas, rainfall has become more erratic, leading to prolonged droughts and dry spells that impact crop and livestock production. Other regions experience heavy rain, flooding, soil erosion, and waterlogging, damaging crops, washing away nutrients, and disrupting planting schedules. For smallholder farmers in rain-fed agricultural systems, these changes in rainfall patterns are particularly disruptive (FAO, 2016).

Increased Frequency of Extreme Weather Events

Due to climate change, the frequency of extreme weather events, such as hurricanes, droughts, floods, and heatwaves, has increased. These events devastate crops, disrupt food production systems, and increase the vulnerability of rural agricultural communities. Extreme events also make infrastructure, such as storage facilities and transportation networks, vulnerable to damage, leading to post-harvest losses and reduced market access for rural farmers.

Soil Degradation and Desertification

Climate change accelerates soil degradation and desertification, especially in arid and semi-arid regions. Rising temperatures and changing rainfall patterns exacerbate soil erosion, nutrient depletion, and salinisation, reducing soil fertility and its capacity to support crop growth. These changes particularly impact smallholder farmers, who may

need more resources to implement soil conservation
practices effectively.

Adaptation Strategies for Smallholder Farmers

Adaptation strategies enable farmers to adjust their agricultural practices to mitigate the impacts of climate change. For smallholder farmers, who may have limited resources, adaptation strategies need to be accessible, practical, and cost-effective. Some essential adaptation practices include diversified cropping, conservation agriculture, and improved crop varieties.

Diversified Cropping Systems

Crop diversification involves growing multiple crops or varieties within the same farming system. Farmers can reduce their dependency on a single crop by diversifying, minimising risk and ensuring more stable income sources. Diversified cropping can also enhance soil fertility and minimise pest and disease pressure. Examples include intercropping (growing two or more crops together, such as maise with legumes) and agroforestry (integrating trees with crops to improve soil health and provide additional resources like fodder and fuelwood).

82

Climate-Resilient Crop Varieties

Adapting to climate impacts directly involves Using drought-tolerant, flood-resistant, or pest-resistant crop varieties. Scientific advancements in plant breeding and biotechnology have enabled the development of crop varieties that are more resilient to specific climate-related challenges. For example, developing drought-tolerant maise helps farmers in arid regions maintain yields during dry spells. Adopting these varieties can increase productivity and reduce crop losses, providing food security even under adverse weather conditions.

Improved Water Management

Efficient water management practices like drip irrigation, water harvesting, and mulching help smallholder farmers optimise water use and reduce dependency on erratic rainfall. Drip irrigation delivers water directly to plant roots and is highly efficient, especially in water-scarce areas. Water harvesting systems, such as ponds or reservoirs, capture and store rainwater during dry periods, enabling farmers to irrigate crops even when rainfall is low.

Soil Conservation Practices

Maintaining soil health is vital for sustainable crop production, as climate change accelerates soil degradation. Practices such as minimum tillage, crop rotation, cover cropping, and using organic fertilisers (compost and manure) help improve soil structure, prevent erosion, and increase nutrient retention. Cover crops, for instance, protect the soil from erosion, add organic matter, and improve moisture retention. These soil conservation practices help build resilience and sustain productivity over time.

Climate Information Services.

Access to accurate climate information, such as weather and seasonal climate predictions, helps smallholder farmers make informed decisions. Mobile applications and local extension services increasingly provide climate-related information, allowing farmers to adjust planting schedules, select appropriate crops, and take preventive measures against anticipated weather events. By knowing about potential climate risks, farmers can better manage their resources and minimise crop losses.

Mitigation Practices, Such as Carbon Sequestration

While adaptation strategies help farmers cope with climate change, mitigation practices aim to reduce agriculture's contribution to greenhouse gas emissions. Essential mitigation practices include carbon sequestration, reduced reliance on synthetic fertilisers, and conservation tillage.

Carbon Sequestration in Soils and Agroforestry

Carbon sequestration captures and stores atmospheric carbon dioxide in plants, soils, and other carbon sinks. Through sustainable land management practices, agriculture can play a role in removing CO_2 from the atmosphere and storing it in plant biomass and soil. Agroforestry, for example, increases tree cover on agricultural land, capturing carbon in trees and roots while enhancing biodiversity and soil health. Soil organic carbon can be increased through cover cropping, organic fertilisation, and reduced tillage, which minimise soil disturbance and improve carbon storage (Lal, 2004).

Reduced Use of Synthetic Fertilizers

Synthetic fertilisers contribute to greenhouse gas emissions by releasing nitrous oxide, a potent greenhouse gas. Reducing fertiliser use or switching to organic fertilisers (e.g., compost, manure) helps lower these emissions. Integrated nutrient management, where fertilisers are used sparingly and supplemented with organic amendments, reduces dependency on synthetic inputs and enhances soil health. Precision agriculture technology can also help farmers apply fertilisers more accurately, minimising waste and emissions.

Conservation Tillage

Conservation tillage is a farming practice that minimises soil disturbance, thus preserving soil structure and enhancing carbon storage. By leaving crop residues on the soil surface and reducing ploughing, conservation tillage helps retain soil organic matter and reduce erosion. It also prevents the release of stored carbon into the atmosphere, mitigating climate change. This practice can improve soil water retention and reduce the need for irrigation, making it a sustainable option for farmers in drought-prone regions.

Use of Renewable Energy Sources

Adopting renewable energy sources, such as solar-powered irrigation systems, wind turbines, and biogas, helps reduce agricultural operations' carbon footprint. Solar irrigation systems, for instance, provide a sustainable alternative to diesel pumps, reducing greenhouse gas emissions and fuel costs. Farmers can reduce their reliance on fossil fuels by integrating renewable energy into their practices and contributing to climate change mitigation.

Examples of Climate-Resilient Agricultural Systems

Climate-resilient agricultural systems can withstand and recover from climate shocks while sustaining productivity. These systems incorporate traditional and innovative practices tailored to specific environmental and socioeconomic conditions.

Agroforestry Systems

Agroforestry combines agriculture and forestry practices, integrating trees, crops, and sometimes livestock on the same land. Trees act as windbreaks, reduce soil erosion, and improve soil fertility through nitrogen-fixing. They also provide shade for crops, helping to reduce soil temperatures and conserve soil moisture. Agroforestry is especially beneficial in areas prone to drought, as trees contribute to water conservation and minimise crop stress (Garrity et al., 2010).

Integrated Crop-Livestock Systems

Crop-livestock integration is a sustainable system that combines crop production with livestock management. Farmers create a closed-loop system that enhances soil fertility and reduces the need for chemical inputs by rotating livestock grazing areas and using livestock manure as a natural fertiliser. This system diversifies farm income, providing resilience during crop failures or market fluctuations.

Conservation Agriculture Systems

Conservation agriculture focuses on minimum soil disturbance, permanent soil cover, and crop rotation. By maintaining soil health, conservation agriculture increases resilience to drought and extreme weather events. Permanent soil cover, achieved through covering crops or mulch, protects the soil from erosion, reduces water loss, and provides habitats for beneficial organisms. This system is widely applicable and offers a practical way for farmers to conserve resources and improve productivity in the face of climate change.

Aquaponics and Hydroponics

Aquaponics and hydroponics are soilless farming systems that combine fish farming with crop cultivation. In aquaponics, fish waste provides nutrients for plants, and plants help filter water for fish, creating an autonomous system. These water-efficient and space-saving systems suit regions with limited arable land and water resources. By reducing dependency on soil and enhancing water efficiency, aquaponics and hydroponics offer climate-resilient options for food production (Love et al., 2015).

CHAPTER 6:

ECONOMIC VIABILITY OF SUSTAINABLE PRACTICES

Sustainable agricultural practices are growing in importance as the world seeks ways to meet food production demands while mitigating environmental impacts. Economic viability is critical to sustainability, ensuring that these practices can be financially feasible for farmers. This research examines the cost-benefit analysis of sustainable vs conventional farming, market access and value chain development for rural farmers, case studies on profitable, sustainable farms, and the role of cooperatives and farmer associations. Additional relevant topics will also be suggested to provide a holistic understanding of economic viability in sustainable agriculture.

1. Cost-Benefit Analysis of Sustainable vs. Conventional Farming

A thorough cost-benefit analysis of sustainable and conventional farming practices highlights their economic, environmental, and social implications. Sustainable agriculture often involves organic farming, integrated pest management (IPM), and crop rotation, focusing on long-term ecological balance rather than short-term profits. By comparison, conventional farming often depends heavily on synthetic fertilisers, pesticides, and monocultures to achieve immediate yield gains, which can deplete natural resources and contribute to environmental degradation.

Initial Investment and Long-Term Returns

Sustainable farming practices may involve higher initial costs, particularly for transitioning from conventional to sustainable systems. For instance, organic certification can be costly, requiring compliance with various standards. However, sustainable practices often lower input costs over time as farmers reduce their dependence on synthetic fertilisers, pesticides, and energy-intensive irrigation systems (Ponisio et al., 2015). The returns from sustainable farming can be consistent and even exceed conventional returns significantly as soil fertility improves, crop resilience strengthens, and market demand for organic products rises.

Risk Reduction and Resilience

Sustainable practices often enhance a farm's resilience to climate-related risks. For instance, organic soil management improves water retention, reducing crop vulnerability to droughts, while diverse cropping systems reduce the risk of total crop failure. By reducing dependency on external inputs, sustainable farms are less vulnerable to price fluctuations in fertiliser and pesticide markets, which can be a significant advantage over conventional farming.

Profit Margins and Consumer Demand

With rising consumer awareness, demand for sustainably produced foods is increasing. Products labelled as "organic," "fair trade," or "sustainably sourced" often command higher prices in the market, leading to better profit margins for farmers. In regions with a well-established market for organic products, such as the European Union and the United States, this demand provides an economic incentive for sustainable practices (Willer & Lernoud, 2019). However, farmers must navigate costs associated with certifications, quality standards, and

marketing strategies to ensure sustainable farming
is economically viable.

2. Market Access and Value Chain Development for Rural Farmers

Access to markets and a well-integrated value chain are essential for rural farmers to ensure that their sustainably grown produce can reach consumers efficiently and profitably. Market access challenges include limited infrastructure, fluctuating prices, and inadequate storage facilities, which can undermine the economic viability of sustainable practices.

Improving Market Access

Market access can be improved through investments in infrastructure, such as roads, storage facilities, and digital connectivity. Rural farmers can benefit from platforms that link producers with buyers directly, reducing intermediaries and increasing farmers' profit share. Digital platforms and mobile applications, such as FarmCrowdy in Nigeria, help farmers access market information, enhancing transparency and reducing exploitation by intermediaries.

Value Chain Development.

95

Value chain development involves strengthening every stage, from production to distribution to end-user consumption. Sustainable value chain development encourages practices that reduce post-harvest losses, such as using renewable energy for cold storage, efficient transportation methods, and processing facilities near farms. For example, establishing processing facilities for organic crops near farming areas can reduce transportation costs and allow farmers to add value to their products (e.g., organic jams and dried fruits).

Access to Fair Trade and Export Markets.

Export markets for sustainable products offer lucrative opportunities, but rural farmers often need support to meet the standards required for international trade. Partnerships with NGOs and government agencies can help farmers obtain necessary certifications, improve packaging, and establish fair-trade connections, making it feasible to access higher-paying foreign markets. Fair-trade accreditation, in particular, ensures farmers receive a premium price, providing an incentive for sustainable practices.

3. Case Studies on Profitable Sustainable Farms

Case studies of profitable, sustainable farms provide insights into how various sustainable practices contribute to economic viability. Examples from different regions highlight diverse approaches that achieve both environmental and financial sustainability.

The Rodale Institute, USA'

Known for its pioneering work in organic farming, the institute has demonstrated that organic practices can yield profits comparable to or exceeding those of conventional agriculture. The institute's research farm showcases composting, cover cropping, and no-till farming, which improve soil health, reduce inputs, and maintain high yields. Over the years, studies conducted at Rodale indicate that organic farms can have higher resilience and profitability, especially in adverse weather (LaSalle & Hepperly, 2008).

Coffee Cooperatives in Ethiopia

Ethiopian coffee farmers using sustainable agroforestry practices integrate shade trees, which improve biodiversity and soil fertility while allowing farmers to sell premium coffee in fair-trade markets. These cooperatives have enabled small-scale farmers to earn higher prices by eliminating intermediaries, improving income stability, and supporting community development projects. This case demonstrates the financial benefits of sustainable practices combined with cooperative organisation and fair-trade certification.

Organic Rice Farming in India

In India, several rice farmers have adopted sustainable practices through the System of Rice Intensification (SRI), which reduces water use and input costs while increasing yields. This system has enabled farmers in water-scarce regions to grow rice profitably, making SRI an attractive, sustainable option for rural farmers facing climate-induced water shortages (Uphoff, 2003). Adopting SRI has provided both environmental and economic benefits, leading to improved livelihoods and more resilient farming systems.

4. Role of Cooperatives and Farmer Associations

Cooperatives and farmer associations play a vital role in making sustainable practices economically viable for smallholder farmers. These organisations support access to resources, training, and markets while strengthening farmers' bargaining power.

Access to Resources and Inputs.

Cooperatives enable smallholder farmers to access subsidised inputs such as organic fertilisers, seeds, and tools. By purchasing inputs in bulk, cooperatives lower costs for individual farmers, making it more feasible to adopt sustainable practices. For example, in Kenya, the Dairy Farmers Association provides members access to quality feed and veterinary services, improving productivity while reducing costs.

Training and Knowledge Exchange

Cooperatives facilitate training programs on sustainable practices such as IPM, crop rotation, and conservation agriculture. These training sessions give farmers the skills and knowledge to implement sustainable practices effectively. Farmer Field Schools (FFS), often organised by cooperatives, provide hands-on training, allowing farmers to learn by doing and adapt practices to their unique local conditions.

Collective Marketing and Enhanced Bargaining Power

Cooperatives strengthen farmers' bargaining power by allowing them to collectively negotiate better prices and terms with buyers. This collective approach reduces reliance on intermediaries and ensures farmers retain a higher share of profits. For example, in Colombia, coffee cooperatives negotiate directly with international buyers, enabling members to sell their organic coffee at premium prices while reinvesting profits into community development.

5. Future research areas

In broadening the study of economic viability in sustainable agriculture, several additional topics provide a more comprehensive understanding:

Access to Credit and Financial Services for Sustainable Farmers

Sustainable practices often require upfront investments, but limited credit access can hinder smallholder farmers' adoption. Microfinance institutions, agricultural banks, and government subsidies can help bridge this gap. Exploring how access to financing options impacts adopting sustainable practices is essential for understanding economic viability.

Policy Incentives for Sustainable Agriculture

Government policies, such as subsidies for organic inputs, tax incentives, and grants for sustainable infrastructure, can support farmers' transitions to sustainable practices. Analysing the impact of policy incentives on the economic viability of sustainable agriculture would reveal how supportive government action can facilitate widespread adoption.

Impact of Climate Change on Economic Viability

Climate change significantly affects the economic viability of both sustainable and conventional farming. Sustainable practices are often more resilient, but understanding how climate change impacts input costs, yields, and market access is crucial for evaluating long-term economic viability.

Certification and Labelling Programs.

Certification and labelling programs, such as organic, fair trade, and Rainforest Alliance, are essential for creating consumer trust and increasing the marketability of sustainable products. However, these programs can be costly to implement and maintain. Analysing certification programs' economic benefits and challenges provides insights into their viability for small-scale sustainable farmers.

Post-Harvest Handling and Processing for Value Addition.

Adding value to sustainable products through processing and proper post-harvest handling can increase profitability. Value-added products like organic fruit jams, dried herbs, and dairy products cater to niche markets, potentially improving income for sustainable farmers. The cost-effectiveness of processing facilities and technologies in rural areas is worth exploring.

Impact of Digital Agriculture on Economic Viability.

Digital technologies, such as mobile apps for market prices, weather forecasting, and virtual training, can improve sustainable practices and economic returns for farmers. Assessing the role of digital agriculture in enhancing economic viability is relevant, especially for smallholder farmers in remote areas.

CHAPTER 7:

SOCIAL AND CULTURAL DIMENSIONS OF SUSTAINABLE AGRICULTURE

Sustainable agriculture is not just an economic and environmental challenge but also deeply embedded in social and cultural contexts. The success of sustainable practices depends on how communities engage with the process, the roles that different groups—such as women, youth, and Indigenous peoples—play in agriculture, and the extent to which traditional knowledge is integrated into modern farming systems. This research explores sustainable agriculture's social and cultural dimensions, focusing on community-based approaches, gender roles, traditional knowledge, and youth involvement.

1. Community-Based Approaches and Stakeholder Engagement

Community-based approaches to sustainable agriculture emphasise the collective effort of all stakeholders in the agricultural system. These approaches focus on engaging local communities, government bodies, NGOs, and the private sector in decision-making and implementation.

Inclusive Decision-Making.

Sustainable agriculture requires the active participation of all community members, particularly when planning and implementing agricultural practices. By involving local farmers, women, youth, and marginalised groups in decision-making processes, agricultural projects become more relevant and tailored to the community's needs. Stakeholder engagement helps ensure that policies and practices are more likely to be adopted, as they are rooted in the community's knowledge and realities.

Cooperative Models

Community-based approaches often rely on collaborative models, where farmers work together to achieve common goals, such as collective buying of inputs, joint marketing of products, and shared access to processing facilities. These models allow farmers to pool resources, reduce costs, and improve bargaining power. In places like Ethiopia and India, community-managed cooperatives have played a critical role in promoting sustainable agriculture by creating stronger ties among farmers and supporting the adoption of eco-friendly practices.

Social Capital and Trust

The success of community-based approaches often depends on social capital—the trust and relationships between community members. Social solid networks within farming communities can facilitate the sharing of information, resources, and labour, making it easier for farmers to adopt sustainable practices and technologies. By fostering relationships of trust, farmers are more likely to collaborate on sustainability initiatives and support one another in the face of challenges.

Participatory Approaches to Extension Services.

Participatory extension services are crucial to promoting sustainable agricultural practices. These services, which involve community members in identifying problems, designing solutions, and implementing projects, are particularly effective in rural areas where conventional top-down extension services may be less successful. Farmers become more confident in adopting new practices and technologies by engaging communities.

2. Gender Roles in Sustainable Agriculture

Gender dynamics play a significant role in the adoption of sustainable agricultural practices. In many societies, women are crucial contributors to agricultural labour but are often excluded from decision-making processes and resource access. Addressing gender inequalities is critical for achieving sustainable agriculture and ensuring that both men and women can benefit from the economic, environmental, and social opportunities that sustainable farming provides.

Women's Contribution to Agriculture.

Women comprise a significant portion of the agricultural workforce, particularly in developing countries. In sub-Saharan Africa and South Asia, women often manage smallholder farms, perform labour-intensive tasks such as weeding and harvesting, and are responsible for food processing and marketing. Despite their central role, women frequently face barriers to accessing land, credit, and training in sustainable practices. Addressing these gender-based inequalities is crucial for the effective implementation of sustainable agriculture.

Gendered Impacts of Climate Change.

Climate change disproportionately affects women, particularly in rural areas, where women are the primary caretakers of food production and water management. Due to limited access to resources and decision-making power, women are often more vulnerable to climate-induced challenges, such as droughts and floods. Gender-sensitive approaches to climate-smart agriculture can enhance women's resilience and help them better cope with changing environmental conditions.

Empowerment Through Sustainable Practices.

Promoting women's access to resources such as land, credit, and training in sustainable practices can significantly enhance their empowerment. Gender-sensitive policies in agriculture that encourage women's access to education and skills development are crucial. In rural areas, empowering women to take leadership roles in community organisations or cooperatives can ensure that sustainable agriculture benefits everyone, improving food security and income generation for families.

Equitable Access to Technology and Inputs

Sustainable agricultural technologies, such as drought-resistant crops, organic fertilisers, and water-efficient irrigation systems, can help improve productivity and resilience. However, gender-specific barriers must be addressed so that these technologies benefit women equally. Ensuring women have equal access to information, training, and technology will help close the gender gap in sustainable agriculture.

3. Traditional Knowledge and Indigenous Practices

Indigenous and traditional knowledge is invaluable in sustainable agriculture, as these practices have evolved to cope with local environmental conditions over generations. Many conventional agricultural practices are highly sustainable, relying on local biodiversity, water conservation, and soil fertility management techniques with minimal ecological impact.

Agroecological Practices.

Traditional knowledge often aligns with the principles of agroecology, which integrates ecological principles into farming systems. Practices such as crop rotation, agroforestry, intercropping, and organic fertilisers are rooted in indigenous agricultural knowledge. These practices enhance soil health, improve water retention, and reduce dependency on external inputs. In places like the Andean highlands of South America, indigenous farmers have used these methods for centuries to maintain soil fertility and biodiversity.

Seed Saving and Preservation

Many Indigenous communities have developed rich traditions of saving and exchanging seeds, which enhance crop diversity and resilience. Preserving traditional seed varieties is crucial for maintaining genetic diversity, which can help farmers adapt to changing environmental conditions. Seed banks and community seed-saving initiatives are increasingly recognised as vital tools for promoting sustainable agriculture in the face of climate change.

Cultural and Spiritual Significance

Traditional agricultural practices are often deeply tied to cultural and spiritual beliefs. In many indigenous cultures, farming is seen as a sacred practice closely connected to the land and natural resources. By recognising the cultural importance of these practices, sustainable agriculture can be more effectively implemented in a way that respects local customs and traditions.

Challenges to Preserving Traditional Knowledge.

Losing traditional knowledge is a significant concern as younger generations migrate to cities or adopt more modern farming techniques. Efforts to preserve and integrate traditional knowledge into contemporary farming practices are critical for maintaining agricultural sustainability. Programs that document indigenous farming knowledge and encourage its transmission between generations are essential for the future of sustainable agriculture.

4. Youth Involvement and Succession Planning in Farming

Youth involvement in farming is essential to the long-term sustainability of agriculture. As the older generation retires or moves away from farming, succession planning becomes critical to ensuring the flourishing of sustainable agricultural practices.

Attracting Youth to Agriculture.

Traditionally, farming has been seen as a less attractive career path, especially for young people who often seek opportunities in urban areas. However, the rise of sustainable agriculture offers a chance to revitalise rural farming communities by attracting youth interested in eco-friendly farming practices. Youth involvement can be fostered through education, access to modern technologies, and opportunities for entrepreneurship in agriculture.

Training and Education.

Providing youth with training in sustainable farming practices, business management, and agricultural

114

technologies is vital for ensuring the next generation's participation in agriculture. Agricultural universities and vocational training programs focused on sustainable practices can equip young people with the knowledge and skills to thrive in a sustainable farming system.

Succession Planning

Succession planning is essential to ensuring that family-owned farms remain viable and sustainable. Many farmers need help passing on their farms to the next generation due to economic pressures, lack of interest, or the absence of clear plans for transfer. Developing clear, practical succession plans can help prevent the loss of family farms and ensure that sustainable practices continue to be applied. Encouraging intergenerational knowledge transfer and supporting young farmers in taking on leadership roles can help facilitate this process.

Youth-Led Agricultural Innovation.

Youth are often more open to adopting innovative technologies and practices. They are crucial drivers of change, particularly regarding digital tools such as mobile apps for farm management, access to markets, and information on weather patterns. Supporting youth-led agricultural start-ups and initiatives can encourage the adoption of new technologies in sustainable agriculture.

CHAPTER 8:

POLICIES AND GOVERNANCE FOR SUSTAINABLE RURAL AGRICULTURE

Sustainable rural agriculture requires a comprehensive policy framework that involves multiple stakeholders, including governments, non-governmental organisations (NGOs), international bodies, and private enterprises. These actors play a crucial role in shaping the landscape for sustainable agriculture by implementing policies, providing resources, and fostering collaborations. The right regulatory frameworks and strategic partnerships are essential to promoting sustainable farming practices that ensure food security, economic development, and environmental sustainability.

1. Policies Supporting Sustainable Agriculture

Policies that support sustainable agriculture are designed to foster agricultural practices that are socially inclusive, economically viable, and environmentally responsible. These policies operate at multiple levels, from local to international, and address various issues such as land use, climate change adaptation, biodiversity conservation, and rural livelihoods.

National Agricultural Policies.

Many countries have developed national policies prioritising sustainable farming practices. These policies often focus on increasing agricultural productivity while minimising environmental harm. For example, policies may incentivise adopting environmentally friendly practices like agroforestry, integrated pest management (IPM), and organic farming. In many developing countries, national policies focus on improving soil health, water management, and increasing access to markets for rural farmers.

Climate-Smart Agriculture (CSA) Policies

With climate change's increasing impact on agriculture, CSA policies are gaining traction. These policies promote farming practices that enhance resilience to climate variability and reduce greenhouse gas emissions. CSA involves a combination of adaptation and mitigation strategies, such as drought-resistant crops, water conservation techniques, and carbon sequestration through agroforestry. Governments worldwide are increasingly incorporating CSA principles into their agricultural policies to ensure the long-term sustainability of rural farming communities.

Subsidies and Incentives for Sustainable Practices.

In many countries, governments provide subsidies, tax incentives, and grants to encourage adopting sustainable agricultural practices. These financial incentives can cover the costs of transitioning to organic farming, embracing precision farming technologies, or implementing conservation measures. Such subsidies help offset the initial costs associated with sustainable farming practices and make them more accessible to smallholder farmers.

Land Reform and Tenure Security.

Land tenure policies are critical in ensuring sustainable agriculture. In many developing countries, farmers lack secure land rights, which can discourage long-term investment in soil health and sustainable practices. Land reform policies that provide secure land tenure for farmers can encourage better land stewardship and investment in sustainable farming practices. Secure land tenure also promotes social stability, as farmers are more likely to engage in long-term planning if they have confidence in their land rights.

2. Role of Governments, NGOs, and International Bodies

Governments, NGOs, and international bodies play critical roles in shaping the policies and frameworks that support sustainable agriculture. Each actor has a unique role in promoting sustainable farming practices and ensuring rural development.

Role of Governments.

Governments are the primary policymakers in promoting sustainable agriculture. They establish national agricultural policies, allocate budgets for rural development, and provide the necessary infrastructure for farmers. Governments can implement and enforce laws and regulations that govern land use, water management, and environmental protection. Additionally, governments can invest in research and development (R&D) for sustainable agricultural technologies and practices, provide extension services to farmers, and facilitate access to credit and markets.

Role of NGOs.

NGOs often play an essential role in advocating for sustainable agricultural policies and providing on-the-ground support to rural communities. Many NGOs work directly with farmers to provide training on sustainable farming practices, raise awareness about climate change, and advocate for policy changes that favour rural development. NGOs also often collaborate with international organisations and governments to provide financial assistance, technical expertise, and project implementation support in rural areas.

Role of International Bodies.

International organisations such as the Food and Agriculture Organization (FAO), the World Bank, and the United Nations Environment Programme (UNEP) support sustainable agriculture through international agreements, technical assistance, and funding. These bodies help coordinate efforts to combat global agricultural challenges such as food security, climate change, and rural poverty. They provide valuable data, research, and frameworks that guide national and regional policies on sustainable agriculture.

Multilateral Agreements.

International bodies often facilitate multilateral agreements that set the standards and guidelines for sustainable agriculture practices. For instance, the United Nations' Sustainable Development Goals (SDGs) include targets related to sustainable agriculture, achieving food security and improving rural livelihoods. International agreements like the Paris Climate Agreement also influence national agricultural policies by encouraging countries to reduce emissions and adopt climate-resilient farming practices.

3. Regulatory Frameworks for Organic and Sustainable Products

For sustainable agriculture to be viable in the marketplace, clear regulatory frameworks are needed to govern organic and sustainably produced products' production, certification, and marketing. These frameworks ensure that farmers adhere to specific standards while giving consumers confidence in the integrity of sustainable products.

Organic Certification Standards.

Many countries have established national certification standards defining organic farming. Organic certification ensures that farms adhere to strict guidelines prohibiting synthetic pesticides, chemical fertilisers, and genetically modified organisms (GMOs). These standards help create a market for organic products and assure consumers about organic food's environmental and health benefits. Certification bodies such as the USDA Organic in the United States and the EU Organic label in Europe regulate these standards.

Sustainable Product Labels.

Beyond organic certification, various sustainability certifications exist for products that meet broader environmental, social, and economic criteria. For example, the Rainforest Alliance certification focuses on sustainable farming practices that conserve biodiversity and protect ecosystems. Similarly, Fair Trade certification ensures that farmers are paid a fair price for their products while meeting environmental and social sustainability standards. These labels create a market for sustainably produced goods and help consumers make informed choices.

Regulatory Compliance for Sustainable Practices.

Governments can establish regulatory frameworks that require farmers to comply with sustainability standards across various practices, such as water use, waste management, and soil conservation. Regulations might mandate using specific technologies, such as drip irrigation or conservation tillage, that promote sustainable land management. Compliance with these regulations can be incentivised through financial support, such as subsidies or grants, which lower farmers' barriers to adopting sustainable practices.

Trade Barriers and Sustainability.

International trade policies often impact the ability of farmers in developing countries to access global markets for sustainable products. Some countries impose strict regulations on importing organic or sustainably produced goods, which can serve as a barrier to trade. Governments and international bodies must work to harmonise organic and sustainable product standards to ensure that smallholder farmers can access global markets without facing excessive costs or trade barriers.

4. Public-Private Partnerships in Promoting Rural Development

Public-private partnerships (PPPs) are essential for promoting rural development and sustainable agriculture. These partnerships leverage the strengths and resources of both the public and private sectors to create lasting, impactful solutions to agricultural and rural development challenges.

Collaboration between Governments and Private Sector

Governments and private companies can collaborate to develop policies, infrastructure, and technologies that support sustainable agriculture. For example, the government might incentivise private companies to invest in renewable energy solutions for farms, such as solar-powered irrigation systems. Private companies can bring technological expertise, capital, and innovation, while governments provide the policy and regulatory frameworks to ensure the success of these initiatives.

Rural Development Projects.

PPPs often fund and implement rural development projects that improve rural communities' infrastructure, market access, and social services. For instance, partnerships between governments and private corporations can help build roads, establish cold storage facilities, or improve transportation networks, enabling rural farmers to access larger markets and reduce post-harvest losses.

Investment in Agricultural Research and Development (R&D).

R&D is essential for advancing sustainable agricultural practices. PPPs can facilitate investment in agricultural research by bringing together government funding and private sector expertise. For example, partnerships between universities, research institutions, and private companies can lead to the development of climate-resilient crops, pest-resistant varieties, and new farming technologies that benefit smallholder farmers.

Supporting Smallholder Farmers through Finance.

Access to finance is one of the biggest challenges for smallholder farmers. Public-private partnerships can help bridge this gap by providing microfinance, credit facilities, and investment opportunities that enable farmers to adopt sustainable technologies. Financial institutions can collaborate with governments to design loan products specifically tailored to the needs of smallholder farmers, such as low-interest loans for purchasing organic inputs or implementing water-saving irrigation systems.

CHAPTER 9:

CASE STUDIES OF SUCCESSFUL SUSTAINABLE AGRICULTURE PROJECTS

1. India – Zero Budget Natural Farming (ZBNF)

Overview of the Project.

India has witnessed the rise of Zero Budget Natural Farming (ZBNF), a system introduced by Subhash Palekar. ZBNF is an agricultural practice designed to reduce farmers' financial burden by eliminating costly chemical inputs. This system promotes natural farming techniques for soil health, water conservation, and biodiversity. ZBNF aims to make farming more economically viable, especially for smallholder farmers in India.

Key Features of ZBNF -

Soil Health:

The ZBNF system emphasises organic materials like cow dung, urine, and plant-based concoctions as fertilisers, which help improve the soil's nutrient content and microbial diversity.

Water Conservation:

The ZBNF approach conserves water and protects the soil from degradation by using mulching, rainwater harvesting, and biopesticide application.

Biodiversity:

The system encourages the cultivation of diverse crops instead of monocultures, which helps reduce pest and disease pressure and improve overall soil fertility.

Lessons Learned -

Community Collaboration:

Successful ZBNF projects rely heavily on community-based participation. By forming farmer cooperatives, knowledge-sharing platforms are created where farmers learn from one another, helping scale sustainable practices.

Cost Reduction:

The primary benefit of ZBNF is the significant reduction in input costs, especially regarding chemical fertilisers and pesticides. It makes farming more economically feasible for smallholder farmers.

Cultural Resonance:

ZBNF is deeply rooted in traditional farming practices and aligns well with local customs, making it more acceptable to rural farming communities.

Factors Contributing to Success -

Government Support:

The Indian government has supported ZBNF through subsidies, providing financial assistance for its implementation. Additionally, nationwide campaigns have been held to train farmers in natural farming methods.

Farmer Empowerment:

ZBNF empowers farmers by reducing dependence on external agricultural inputs, fostering a sense of autonomy and resilience in the face of farming challenges.

Adaptability:

The system's flexibility allows it to be adapted to various local conditions and climates, making it suitable for different regions in India.

2. Brazil – Agroforestry Systems in the Amazon

Overview of the Project –

In Brazil, agroforestry systems have been introduced to the Amazon region to promote sustainable agricultural practices while conserving forests. These systems involve cultivating crops alongside trees, which benefits both agriculture and the environment by preventing deforestation, improving soil health, and promoting biodiversity.

Key Features of Agroforestry Systems -

Multi-layered Cropping:

Agroforestry systems use a variety of plants at different levels, from ground crops to trees, which work in synergy to maximise land use and enhance ecological benefits.

132

Soil Fertility:

Trees in agroforestry systems improve soil fertility through organic matter decomposition and nitrogen fixation, creating a more sustainable farming environment.

Climate Resilience:

Agroforestry systems are highly resilient to extreme weather conditions such as droughts or heavy rainfall, as the diversity of crops and trees helps maintain balance in the ecosystem.

Lessons Learned -

Diversification Reduces Risk:

 Agroforestry diversifies farmers' sources of income, making them less vulnerable to market fluctuations or crop failure. The system can generate profits from both crops and timber.

Ecosystem Services:

Agroforestry provides vital ecosystem services, including soil protection, carbon sequestration, and water filtration, all contributing to environmental sustainability.

Community Involvement:

Successful agroforestry implementation requires the active involvement of local communities, particularly in planning and decision-making. This ensures that the practices are culturally appropriate and feasible.

Factors Contributing to Success -

Policy Support:

Brazil's government has provided a conducive policy environment for agroforestry, including incentives for sustainable land management and forest conservation.

Education and Training:

Extension services and farmer education are crucial for spreading knowledge about the benefits of agroforestry and teaching farmers how to integrate it into their agricultural systems.

Market Access:

Successful agroforestry projects have linked farmers with local and international markets, ensuring they can sell their crops and timber at competitive prices.

Kenya – The Greenbelt Movement.

Overview of the Project –

The Greenbelt Movement, founded by Wangari Maathai in Kenya, is a highly successful environmental organisation focused on tree planting, community empowerment, and sustainable agriculture. The initiative has made significant strides in combating soil erosion, deforestation, and climate change in rural Kenya, especially among women traditionally excluded from land-based decision-making.

Key Features of the Greenbelt Movement -

Tree Planting Initiatives:

The Greenbelt Movement has led to the planting of over 50 million trees in Kenya, improving soil fertility and reversing deforestation.

Sustainable Agriculture Promotion:

The movement encourages farmers to adopt sustainable agricultural practices such as water conservation, agroforestry, organic farming, and tree planting.

Women's Empowerment:

The Greenbelt Movement's central focus is empowering women, particularly in rural areas, by involving them in environmental conservation efforts and enabling them to make land-use decisions.

Lessons Learned -

Gender Empowerment:

The Greenbelt Movement has improved the social fabric of communities and enhanced local agricultural practices by empowering women and involving them in environmental conservation.

Long-Term Commitment:

Sustainable agricultural and environmental projects require a long-term commitment, as benefits such as soil fertility and biodiversity restoration take years to materialise fully.

Collaborative Approach:

Successful projects in Kenya have shown that when local communities, governments, and NGOs collaborate, the initiative is more likely to succeed long-term and be sustainable.

Factors Contributing to Success -

Strong Leadership:

Wangari Maathai's leadership, which advocated for sustainability nationally and globally, was crucial in attracting support and international recognition for the Greenbelt Movement.

Community Ownership:

The Greenbelt Movement's grassroots, community-driven nature has been central to its success, as local communities are the main drivers of its activities.

International Support:

The movement benefited from international funding and support from various NGOs and global environmental organisations, which helped scale its activities.

3. Australia – The Land Care Movement.

Overview of the Project –

The Land Care Movement in Australia is a community-driven initiative focusing on sustainable land management practices. It aims to enhance environmental quality by promoting conservation techniques, such as rotational grazing, reforestation, and soil erosion control. Land care has effectively empowered farmers and landholders to adopt more sustainable farming practices and engage in cooperative land management.

Key Features of Land Care -

Community-Based Action:

Land care emphasises collaboration among farmers, landholders, and other stakeholders to address land degradation and implement sustainable farming techniques.

Sustainable Land Management:

The movement promotes rotational grazing, integrated pest management, and erosion control to improve soil health and increase productivity.

Biodiversity Conservation:

Land care aims to restore native vegetation and protect wildlife habitats, ensuring that agricultural practices are environmentally sustainable.

Lessons Learned -

Collaboration is Key:

Land care's success lies in the active participation of farmers, local governments, and environmental groups. Collaborative decision-making ensures that solutions are tailored to local needs and conditions.

Ongoing Education:

Educating farmers and landowners about the long-term benefits of sustainable practices and providing them with practical tools has been essential for the movement's success.

Monitoring and Adaptation:

Land care has demonstrated the importance of monitoring environmental outcomes and adjusting strategies based on new knowledge and changing conditions.

Factors Contributing to Success -

Government Support:

The Australian government has provided funding, incentives, technical expertise, and resources for land care projects.

Strong Community Networks:

The movement's grassroots nature and the strong community networks it fosters have been crucial to its widespread adoption and long-term success.

Public Awareness:

Land care has raised awareness among farmers and the general public about the need for sustainable land management and environmental stewardship.

4. United States – The Sustainable Agriculture
Research and Education (SARE) Program

Overview of the Project –

The SARE program in the United States is a comprehensive initiative to promote sustainable farming practices through research, education, and outreach. The program supports farmers, ranchers, and agricultural professionals by providing grants for research and developing innovative, sustainable farming practices.

Key Features of SARE -

Research and Innovation:

The program funds research into sustainable farming techniques, such as crop rotation, organic farming, and agroecology, to develop innovative solutions to farming challenges.

Farmer Education:

SARE provides training and educational opportunities to farmers, extension agents, and other agricultural professionals to promote the adoption of sustainable practices.

Farmer-to-Farmer Learning:

The program emphasises the importance of farmer-to-farmer education, enabling farmers to learn from each other's experiences and adopt new practices on their farms.

Lessons Learned -

Research-Driven Solutions:

SARE's success demonstrates the importance of linking research with practical, on-the-ground solutions for farmers. By funding real-world research, SARE has created tangible benefits for agricultural communities.

Community-Based Learning:

The program's emphasis on peer-to-peer learning ensures that the solutions developed are relevant to the needs of local farmers and are more likely to be adopted.

Long-Term Sustainability:

By providing farmers with the tools and knowledge to make sustainable changes, SARE has contributed to the long-term sustainability of American agriculture.

Factors Contributing to Success -

Collaboration with Academia:

SARE works closely with universities and research institutions, ensuring that the research it funds is scientifically rigorous and practical.

Financial Support:

The program provides critical financial support for farmers to experiment with and adopt sustainable practices, reducing the economic risks of transitioning from conventional to sustainable farming methods.

Policy Integration:

SARE's work is aligned with national agricultural policies that emphasise sustainability and innovation, ensuring solid governmental support for the program.

Roadmap to Sustain Agriculture in Rural Development

CHAPTER 10:

FUTURE DIRECTIONS FOR SUSTAINABLE AGRICULTURE IN RURAL DEVELOPMENT

Sustainable agriculture plays a critical role in addressing the challenges of food security, climate change, economic stability, and rural development. As the world faces increasing pressures from a growing population, resource scarcity, and environmental degradation, it is essential to chart a course for future agricultural practices that promote sustainability and resilience. The future of sustainable agriculture in rural development lies in leveraging emerging technologies, scaling successful models, exploring new areas for research and innovation, and fostering a shared vision for a sustainable and resilient agricultural future.

1. Emerging Trends and Technologies

Technological advancements that improve efficiency, reduce environmental impacts, and enhance farming systems' productivity will drive sustainable agriculture's future. These innovations

146

are poised to revolutionise agricultural practices and provide sustainable solutions for rural development.

Precision Agriculture:

Precision agriculture is transforming how farmers manage their crops by using advanced technologies like GPS, sensors, and satellite imagery to optimise resources such as water, fertilisers, and pesticides. This data-driven approach helps farmers apply the right amount of inputs at the right time, reducing waste and improving productivity while minimising environmental harm. Precision agriculture has the potential to significantly reduce costs and increase yields, especially in areas where resource use is inefficient.

Genetic Engineering and Biotechnology:

Biotechnology holds great promise for sustainable agriculture by developing genetically modified (GM) crops more resistant to pests, diseases, and adverse weather conditions. Crops that require fewer chemical inputs and are drought-tolerant can help ensure food security in areas increasingly vulnerable to climate change. CRISPR gene-editing technologies also improve crop resilience and enhance nutritional content.

Vertical Farming and Urban Agriculture:

With increasing urbanisation and limited arable land, vertical farming and urban agriculture are emerging as viable options for sustainable food production. These methods involve growing crops in stacked layers or urban environments, using minimal land and water while reducing the carbon footprint of transportation. Technologies like hydroponics and aquaponics allow for high-efficiency food production with fewer resources, making them particularly suitable for densely populated urban areas and regions with scarce agricultural land.

Artificial Intelligence and Machine Learning:

AI and machine learning are becoming integral in sustainable agriculture. AI algorithms can analyse large datasets from various sources, such as soil sensors and weather patterns, to predict crop performance and optimise farming decisions. AI-powered systems can also automate pest detection, crop monitoring, and irrigation management, improving efficiency and reducing labour costs.

Biological Pest Control:

Biological pest control uses natural predators, parasites, or pathogens to manage pest populations as an alternative to chemical pesticides. This method reduces the reliance on harmful chemicals and promotes biodiversity, helping protect beneficial insects and soil health. Integrated pest management (IPM) systems, which combine biological pest control with other sustainable practices, are gaining traction as effective strategies for pest management in sustainable farming systems.

Blockchain for Transparency and Traceability:

Blockchain technology is increasingly used in agriculture to ensure transparency, traceability, and accountability in food supply chains. By enabling secure, decentralised records of farming practices, production, and distribution, blockchain helps ensure that sustainable farming practices are followed and that consumers can access accurate information

about the origins and sustainability of the food they
purchas

2. Scaling Up Successful Models

While innovative approaches to sustainable agriculture are emerging, one of the biggest challenges remains scaling up successful models to achieve widespread adoption and impact. Sustainable agricultural models can improve food security, economic livelihoods, and rural development.

Policy Support and Incentives:

Scaling up successful sustainable agriculture models requires strong policy support at national and international levels. Governments must implement policies that incentivise sustainable practices, such as subsidies for organic farming, financial support for farmers transitioning to sustainable systems, and regulation of environmentally harmful agricultural practices. Ensuring access to funding and technical support for smallholder farmers can help scale up successful models in rural areas.

Farmer Cooperatives and Networks:

151

Farmer cooperatives play a crucial role in scaling sustainable agriculture by providing collective support and creating economies of scale for smallholder farmers. By joining cooperatives, farmers can access better markets, share resources and knowledge, and benefit from bulk purchasing of inputs. Expanding the use of cooperatives and networks that promote sustainable practices can help drive the widespread adoption of sustainable agriculture.

Training and Education Programs:

Scaling sustainable agriculture practices also requires comprehensive education and training programs for farmers, especially in rural areas. Extension services, workshops, and online courses can give farmers the knowledge and skills to adopt new sustainable technologies and practices. Peer-to-peer learning and farmer-to-farmer networks also effectively share expertise and scale successful models in rural communities.

Corporate Partnerships:

Corporate partnerships can provide the resources and expertise needed to scale sustainable agriculture, especially with agribusinesses and food processors. Companies can play a pivotal role in promoting sustainable farming practices through supply chain integration, offering financial incentives for farmers to adopt sustainable practices, and facilitating market access for sustainable products. By collaborating with local communities, these partnerships can create a more sustainable and resilient agricultural system.

Global Initiatives and Collaboration:

Successful sustainable agriculture models can be scaled through international collaboration and global initiatives. For example, the United Nations' Sustainable Development Goals (SDGs) emphasise the importance of sustainable agriculture and encourage nations to share knowledge, technology, and resources. Multinational organisations, non-governmental organisations (NGOs), and international development agencies can support scaling efforts by providing financial resources, technical expertise, and platforms for collaboration.

3. Potential Areas for Research and Innovation

As sustainable agriculture continues to evolve, numerous opportunities exist for further research and innovation. Research can be crucial in developing new technologies, practices, and strategies that enhance sustainability in farming and rural development.

Climate-Smart Agriculture:

Further research is needed to develop climate-smart agriculture practices that enhance the resilience of farming systems to climate change. It includes researching drought-tolerant crops, water-efficient irrigation techniques, and innovative soil management practices. Understanding how climate change affects different agricultural systems and developing adaptive strategies is essential for ensuring that rural communities can thrive in environmental challenges.

Soil Health and Regeneration:

Soil health is the foundation of sustainable agriculture. Research into soil regeneration techniques, such as biochar, composting, and agroecological practices, is critical for improving soil fertility and reducing soil degradation. Developing new technologies and practices that promote soil health can help increase agricultural productivity while minimising environmental harm.

Water Management Innovations:

Water scarcity is one of the biggest challenges for agriculture, especially in arid regions. Innovations in water management, such as intelligent irrigation systems, water harvesting techniques, and wastewater recycling, are crucial for improving water use efficiency in agriculture. Research into drought-resistant crops and soil moisture retention methods will also play a key role in ensuring farmers can access reliable water resources.

Nutrient Management:

The efficient use of nutrients is essential for sustainable crop production. Research into organic fertilisers, nutrient cycling, and low-input farming practices can help reduce the reliance on synthetic fertilisers while maintaining soil fertility. Developing nutrient management strategies that are tailored to local conditions will be vital to achieving sustainable and productive farming systems.

Social and Economic Impact of Sustainable Practices:

There is a growing need for research on adopting sustainable agriculture practices' social and economic impacts. Understanding the benefits of sustainability on rural livelihoods, community health, and gender equity can provide valuable insights for policymakers, NGOs, and agricultural practitioners. Research into market access, fair trade, and the role of cooperatives can also help strengthen the economic viability of sustainable agriculture in rural areas.

4. Vision for Sustainable Agriculture and Rural Resilience

The future of sustainable agriculture lies in creating a vision that ensures environmental sustainability and fosters economic and social resilience in rural communities. A sustainable agricultural system should be one that:

Supports Biodiversity:

A resilient agricultural system promotes biodiversity by protecting ecosystems, ensuring healthy soils, and conserving water. It supports plant and animal species and integrates them into farming practices, maintaining ecological balance while producing food.

Fosters Social Inclusion:

Sustainable agriculture must prioritise social equity, ensuring that marginalised groups, such as women, youth, and indigenous communities, are empowered to participate in decision-making and benefit from the opportunities created by sustainable farming.

Is Economically Viable:

To achieve sustainability, agricultural practices must be economically viable for farmers. This means providing them with access to markets, fair pricing, financial support, and education. Farmers must generate sufficient income while adopting sustainable practices that benefit their livelihoods and the environment.

Addresses Climate Change:

An essential vision for the future of sustainable agriculture is to build systems that are both climate-resilient and capable of mitigating climate change. It includes developing sustainable farming practices that absorb carbon, reduce greenhouse gas emissions, and increase the resilience of farming systems to extreme weather events.

Are Technology-Driven and Innovative:

The future of sustainable agriculture will involve adopting new technologies that increase resource efficiency, improve crop yields, and reduce environmental impacts. From digital tools to precision farming techniques, technology will play a central role in shaping the future of rural development.

CHAPTER 11:

GLOBAL AND REGIONAL POLICY FRAMEWORKS FOR SUSTAINABLE DEVELOPMENT

International agreements are crucial in shaping global policies that drive sustainable agricultural practices, supporting a harmonious balance between development and environmental stewardship. Various global organisations such as the United Nations (UN), the World Trade Organization (WTO), and the Food and Agriculture Organization (FAO) work together with governments to create frameworks that promote sustainable agriculture on a global scale.

International agreements and frameworks.

1. United Nations (UN) and the Sustainable Development Goals (SDGs)

The United Nations' 2030 Agenda for Sustainable Development includes 17 Sustainable Development Goals (SDGs), with Goal 2 specifically focused on ending hunger, achieving food security, improving nutrition, and promoting sustainable agriculture. The goal recognises the importance of agriculture for food security, income, and livelihoods and underscores the need to transform agricultural systems globally to be sustainable. Sustainable agriculture is embedded in multiple SDGs, including those related to climate action (SDG 13), life on land (SDG 15), and poverty reduction (SDG 1).

UN Framework:

The UN supports sustainable agriculture through protocols, conventions, and initiatives, including the UN Framework Convention on Climate Change (UNFCCC), which promotes climate-smart agriculture.

FAO Initiatives:

The FAO, a specialised agency of the UN, guides countries toward more sustainable agricultural practices. It promotes international standards such as agroecology and climate-smart Agriculture and advocates for policies that ensure food security while minimising environmental degradation.

2. The World Trade Organization (WTO)

The WTO plays a significant role in shaping agricultural trade policies globally. Through its Agriculture Agreement, the WTO encourages member countries to reduce agricultural subsidies that distort trade, pushing for more sustainable farming practices in global markets. The WTO's approach is rooted in the belief that trade liberalisation can drive efficiency and sustainability in agriculture by promoting best practices and competition.

Trade and Sustainability:

The WTO also negotiates and creates policies to facilitate the market access of sustainable agricultural products. Issues like eco-labelling and sustainable certification schemes have been discussed, with the organisation working to standardise international regulations and enhance consumer confidence in sustainable agricultural products.

Sustainability in Trade:

The WTO has become more attuned to environmental sustainability issues in recent years, incorporating discussions on green trade and the green economy, which ties sustainable agriculture with economic growth.

3. FAO's Role in International Governance of Agriculture

The United Nations Food and Agriculture Organization (FAO)

This helps member countries develop sustainable agricultural policies addressing food security, resource conservation, and climate change. Through its Strategic Framework, the FAO promotes policies that enhance agricultural productivity while protecting environmental resources, advocating for organic farming, agroforestry, and integrated pest management.

FAO Voluntary Guidelines:

FAO has developed voluntary guidelines for agricultural policies, such as the Voluntary Guidelines on the Responsible Governance of Tenure of Land, Fisheries, and Forests in the

Context of National Food Security, which influences national land-use policies and Sustainable agricultural practices.

Global Platforms:

The FAO's International Treaty on Plant Genetic Resources for Food and Agriculture (ITPGRFA) and Global Soil Partnership (GSP) aim to protect genetic biodiversity and soil health globally and form international frameworks for sustainable agricultural practices.

4. Convention on Biological Diversity (CBD)

The CBD, through its Nagoya Protocol, influences agricultural biodiversity policies worldwide. This framework encourages nations to adopt policies that conserve the biodiversity of farming systems. By promoting biodiversity, the CBD directly links sustainable agriculture with preserving ecosystems vital to agriculture, including pollinators and soil health.

Regional Cooperation and Collaboration

Regional cooperation among countries plays a critical role in facilitating the adoption of sustainable agricultural practices. Different regions have established organisations that foster knowledge exchange, policy alignment, market integration, and shared resources, all contributing to regional sustainable agricultural development. Here are key examples of regional bodies involved in promoting sustainable agriculture:

1. African Union (AU) and the Comprehensive Africa Agriculture Development Programme (CAADP)

The African Union (AU), through its CAADP initiative, works with African governments to transform agriculture across the continent by focusing on sustainable practices that enhance productivity, food security, and economic growth. It is done by creating policies that promote investments in agricultural infrastructure, technology, and sustainable land management practices.

CAADP's Pillars:

The initiative supports sustainable agriculture by focusing on sustainable land and water management, diversification, and climate-smart agricultural practices.

African Green Revolution:

Through initiatives such as the Alliance for a Green Revolution in Africa (AGRA), the AU promotes the integration of smallholder farmers into sustainable value chains and supports environmentally friendly farming practices to increase food production across the continent.

2. ASEAN (Association of Southeast Asian Nations) and the ASEAN Integrated Food Security Framework

The ASEAN region, consisting of Southeast Asian countries, has embraced sustainable agriculture through the ASEAN Integrated Food Security (AIFS) Framework. This framework addresses food security issues while promoting environmentally sustainable agricultural practices. ASEAN encourages regional cooperation through collective action, data sharing, and harmonised policies on food security and agricultural sustainability.

Regional Cooperation on Climate Change:

ASEAN countries work together to implement climate-smart agricultural practices and disaster risk reduction strategies to mitigate climate change's effects on agriculture.

ASEAN's Sustainable Agricultural Initiatives:

The region promotes sustainable farming techniques across its member states, such as agroforestry, organic farming, and integrated pest management through programs like the ASEAN Sustainable Agrifood Systems.

3. Latin American and the Caribbean: The Agricultural Council of the Americas (CAA)

The CAA is a cooperative regional body dedicated to advancing sustainable agriculture across Latin America and the Caribbean. The organisation integrates environmental sustainability into agricultural policies and practices while addressing food security and rural development challenges.

Sustainable Agricultural Policies:

The CAA fosters regional policy dialogue on issues like agricultural trade and climate change adaptation. These initiatives support sustainable farming practices and encourage governments to adopt eco-friendly policies and regulations.

Agro-Ecological Practices:

Through regional cooperation, the body promotes agroecological practices, sustainable land management, and natural resource conservation, improving smallholder access to sustainable farming methods.

4. European Union (EU) and the Common Agricultural Policy (CAP)

The European Union (EU) has established the Common Agricultural Policy (CAP), which provides financial incentives to support sustainable agricultural practices across its member states. The CAP aims to create a more sustainable food production system by promoting organic farming, biodiversity conservation, and climate change adaptation in rural areas.

Greening Measures:

CAP incentivises the adoption of environmental practices such as crop rotation, permanent pasture maintenance, and biodiversity protection through greening measures that prioritise sustainability for EU farmers.

EU Organic Regulation:

The EU has one of the world's largest markets for organic products, and its policies support the growth of the organic sector by setting stringent standards and regulations for organic farming practices.

5. The Pacific Islands: Pacific Islands Forum (PIF)

The Pacific Islands Forum brings together 18 countries and territories in the Pacific to address agricultural sustainability in the face of climate change. The forum supports implementing environmentally friendly and economically viable sustainable agriculture practices, particularly for small island nations heavily dependent on agriculture for livelihoods.

Climate-Resilient Agriculture:

The PIF promotes climate-smart agriculture by implementing drought-tolerant crops, water conservation, and sustainable fisheries management to increase resilience to climate impacts.

Regional Integration:

The PIF fosters regional cooperation by encouraging shared research and knowledge, facilitating agricultural policy alignment, and improving market access to sustainable farm products in the region.

CHAPTER 12:

EDUCATION AND CAPACITY BUILDING IN RURAL AREAS

Education and capacity building are crucial components for advancing sustainable agricultural practices and improving the overall well-being of rural communities. The development of these areas can be accelerated by equipping farmers and rural populations with the necessary skills, knowledge, and access to technology. Below are critical areas for capacity building in rural areas related to agriculture:

1. Building Human Capital in Rural Communities

Human capital refers to individuals' skills, knowledge, and experience in a community that can be utilised for agricultural and economic development. Building human capital in rural areas involves improving the education system, training programs, and technical support services that can enhance agricultural productivity and rural livelihoods.

A. Role of Education in Agricultural Development

Education is vital in improving agricultural practices, empowering rural communities, and promoting sustainable development. Education systems should integrate agricultural knowledge into curricula at all levels, including primary, secondary, and higher education. Rural schools and universities can offer specialised programs in agricultural sciences, sustainable farming practices, and agribusiness management to equip future generations with the tools needed for rural development.

Integration of Agriculture into Formal Education:

Incorporating agricultural subjects into formal education curricula ensures that young people are prepared to participate in agricultural activities in the future. Courses in agronomy, sustainable farming, animal husbandry, and agroforestry are essential in developing knowledge-based solutions.

Vocational Education and Training (VET):

VET programs can train young individuals in practical farming skills, business management, and rural enterprise. Such programs should provide

opportunities for hands-on training and internships in
real-world agricultural settings.

B. Technical Training and Farmer Extension Services

Farmer extension services are essential for delivering technical knowledge to farmers and rural communities. These services can bridge the knowledge gap between farmers and research institutions, providing up-to-date information on sustainable farming practices, pest management, crop diversification, and soil health.

Government and NGO Involvement:

Governments and NGOs can collaborate to create context-specific extension services relevant to local farming systems. Extension workers can visit farms, advise on improving farming methods, and organise workshops on various aspects of agricultural production.

Technical Workshops and Demonstration Farms:

Demonstration farms serve as practical learning hubs where farmers can see sustainable practices in action. Workshops and field days can provide opportunities for farmers to interact with experts, exchange knowledge, and learn about new agricultural innovations.

C. Farmer Education through Knowledge Sharing Platforms

Farmer organisations, cooperatives, and community groups can provide educational opportunities by creating peer-to-peer learning networks. These groups can share experiences, collaborate on research projects, and learn from successful agricultural models. Knowledge sharing fosters the development of local solutions tailored to the specific challenges farmers face in their regions.

Farmer Field Schools (FFS):

These schools use participatory learning methods, where farmers actively engage in hands-on activities, including problem-solving and decision-making, based on local experiences and practices.

2. Adult Learning and Extension Models

Adult learning provides opportunities for older generations in rural areas, especially farmers, to acquire new skills, update their knowledge, and adopt better farming techniques. Non-formal education models are essential in rural settings, where formal schooling may be less accessible, and the need for practical, on-the-ground knowledge is higher.

A. Non-Formal Education Models for Rural Farmers

Non-formal education is often more practical and flexible, allowing farmers to learn at their own pace, in their community context, and with direct relevance to their work. Non-formal education systems include workshops, mobile learning programs, community centres, and radio-based learning.

Mobile Learning Platforms:

Mobile-based education platforms can be an effective means of delivering knowledge to farmers. These platforms can provide short videos, audio

175

clips, and text-based materials in local languages, making them accessible to illiterate or semi-literate farmers.

Community Radio Programs:

In many rural areas, community radio effectively reaches large audiences with information. Radio programs can cover crop management, weather forecasts, market prices, and best farming practices.

Workshops and Peer Learning:

Local workshops and farmer-to-farmer exchanges are powerful tools for sharing knowledge and skills. Farmers can learn from their peers through these informal channels and incorporate innovative farming techniques into their practices.

B. Farmer-to-Farmer Extension

The farmer-to-farmer extension model encourages experienced farmers to share their knowledge with less experienced peers. This model focuses on participatory learning and local knowledge, ensuring that the lessons are relevant to the local context and that they respect traditional farming practices.

Mentorship Programs:

Experienced farmers can be paired with younger or less experienced farmers to offer mentorship, advice, and support. It can include technical guidance on specific crops or farming systems, business strategies, and sustainability practices.

Farmer Field Schools:

As mentioned earlier, Farmer Field Schools are among the most successful non-formal education models. They are designed to enable farmers to experiment, learn, and make decisions based on real-life challenges they face on their farms.

C. Community Engagement and Empowerment

Community-based extension programs engage the entire community in learning processes. By focusing on collective decision-making and problem-solving, these models can improve agricultural practices, enhance social capital, and increase the adoption of sustainable practices.

Collective Learning Approaches:

By engaging entire communities in group activities, such as agricultural cooperatives or women's farming groups, collective learning enhances the social fabric of rural areas while providing education that meets the specific needs of farmers.

3. Technology Literacy for Farmers

As agriculture increasingly embraces technology, improving digital literacy among farmers is crucial. Access to mobile technologies, digital tools, and the internet can transform rural agriculture by enhancing farmers' access to information, markets, and agricultural resources.

A. Importance of Digital Literacy in Agriculture

Digital literacy in agriculture refers to farmers' ability to use digital tools such as smartphones, tablets, and computers to access agricultural knowledge, market prices, and weather updates. Digital literacy also involves using mobile applications and software for record-keeping, financial planning, and tracking agrarian production.

Mobile Technology and Applications:

Many mobile applications are designed to help farmers access information on crop management, pest control, soil health, and irrigation. These apps provide real-time data and allow farmers to make informed decisions, boosting productivity and sustainability.

E-Learning Platforms:

Online courses and e-learning platforms can also help farmers learn new techniques, understand climate change impacts, and adapt to market trends. These platforms often provide affordable, accessible learning opportunities tailored to rural needs.

B. Access to Information and Market Integration

Improving technology literacy helps farmers stay updated on the latest agricultural trends, which is particularly important in rural settings where information dissemination can be limited. Access to information through mobile phones and other digital tools allows farmers to integrate into wider agricultural markets, improving market access and reducing dependency on intermediaries.

Weather Forecasting and Climate Information:

Access to mobile applications that provide weather forecasts and climate information is critical for farmers. Knowing when to plant or harvest based on weather predictions can increase crop yield and reduce losses from adverse weather conditions.

Digital Marketplaces:

Digital platforms that connect farmers directly with buyers reduce the reliance on intermediaries and improve market access. These platforms allow farmers to sell their products reasonably, potentially increasing their income.

C. Bridging the Digital Divide

One of the challenges in increasing technology literacy is ensuring equitable access to digital tools and infrastructure. Rural areas often need more internet access and high smartphone costs. Bridging the digital divide is essential to ensure that all farmers, regardless of location or socio-economic status, can benefit from technological advancements.

Public-Private Partnerships for Connectivity:

Governments and private sector companies can collaborate to expand internet infrastructure in rural areas, provide affordable smartphones, and establish community hubs where farmers can access technology and learn how to use it.

Digital Literacy Training:

Training programs on basic computer skills, internet use, and mobile phone applications are essential for increasing technology literacy in rural areas. These programs should be practical, easy to understand, and tailored to the needs of farmers with varying levels of digital expertise.

CHAPTER 13:

RURAL INFRASTRUCTURE FOR SUSTAINABLE DEVELOPMENT

Rural infrastructure plays a pivotal role in supporting sustainable development by providing the necessary services and facilities that enable rural communities to thrive economically, socially, and environmentally. In agriculture, infrastructure improvement is vital to increasing productivity, reducing post-harvest losses, and promoting economic growth. Here, we will explore three main areas of rural infrastructure development: transportation and logistics, post-harvest technology and storage, and access to renewable energy.

1. Transportation and Logistics

Efficient transportation networks and logistics systems are vital for rural development, especially in agriculture, where timely access to markets, supplies, and services can directly affect the profitability and sustainability of farming. Rural areas often face transportation challenges that hinder farmers' access to markets, increase transportation costs, and lead to wasted agricultural produce due to delays.

A. Improving Rural Transport Networks

The first step in improving rural transport infrastructure is upgrading rural roads to ensure farmers can easily transport their produce to markets. Many rural areas are isolated due to poor road networks, which leads to increased costs, reduced market access, and, in some cases, the inability to sell produce at its peak market price.

Road Construction and Maintenance:

Governments and development organisations can prioritise constructing and maintaining rural roads to ensure that produce can be moved efficiently from farm to market. It includes improving rural access roads, bridges, and critical transport routes to reduce delays in supply chains.

Affordable Transport Services:

Supporting rural transportation companies or cooperatives specialising in agricultural products can provide affordable transport services for farmers. These services can ensure that produce is transported safely and at affordable rates.

Transport Innovations for Remote Areas:

In areas where traditional vehicles cannot reach, innovations such as small-scale, all-terrain vehicles or even drones for smaller items can be explored to overcome the geographic barriers to market access.

B. Efficient Logistics and Supply Chain Management

Rural logistics and supply chain systems often need to be developed, leading to inefficiencies, higher costs, and post-harvest losses. Improving these systems is critical for ensuring that agricultural products reach consumers promptly and cost-effectively.

Cold Chain Logistics:

Creating or improving cold chain logistics can help preserve quality and reduce waste while transporting perishable goods like fruits, vegetables, dairy, and meat. It involves refrigerated trucks, storage facilities, and packing systems.

Market Linkages and Cooperatives:

Strengthening linkages between farmers and market outlets through cooperatives, agricultural fairs, and digital marketplaces can streamline logistics and ensure a more direct and fair distribution of produce.

Digital Platforms for Supply Chain Coordination:

Technologies such as mobile apps or blockchain can be used to track the movement of goods, optimise routes, and reduce inefficiencies in the supply chain. These tools can help farmers and suppliers communicate better and access real-time information on market prices, transport availability, and logistics.

2. Post-Harvest Technology and Storage

Post-harvest management is critical for reducing food waste, enhancing food security, and ensuring that agricultural products are preserved for longer shelf lives. More post-harvest infrastructure and better storage conditions in rural areas often lead to significant losses of valuable farm produce.

A. Post-Harvest Losses

Globally, it is estimated that about one-third of food produced for human consumption is lost or wasted annually, with post-harvest losses being a significant contributor to this problem, particularly in rural regions. For rural farmers, adequate storage facilities, limited knowledge of handling techniques, and efficient processing methods lead to considerable losses, especially in perishable crops.

Impact on Food Security:

Post-harvest losses affect food availability and lead to income loss for farmers, diminishing the economic viability of farming in rural areas.

Seasonal Fluctuations and Market Access:

Proper storage can allow farmers to hold their produce during off-seasons, enabling them to sell products at higher market prices and thus increasing profitability.

Roadmap to Sustain Agriculture
in Rural Development

B. Innovative Solutions for Preserving and Storing Produce

New technologies and storage methods are being developed and implemented to reduce post-harvest losses, particularly in rural areas with limited resources.

Improved Storage Facilities:

Developing affordable and efficient storage facilities such as silos, cold storage, and airtight storage bags can preserve the quality of crops and prevent spoilage. These storage technologies help keep produce in good condition for longer, reducing waste and enabling farmers to store their goods until market prices are more favourable.

Solar-Powered Refrigeration:

Solar-powered refrigeration units can provide a reliable and sustainable way to store perishable goods like dairy, fruits, and vegetables in remote rural areas where electricity may be unavailable or unreliable. It also reduces the need for fuel-based refrigeration, which is costly and harmful to the environment.

Drying and Processing Technologies:

Drying technologies, such as solar dryers, can help preserve crops like grains, fruits, and herbs by removing excess moisture, which prevents mould growth and spoilage. Farmers can also be trained in small-scale food processing to add value to their produce, making it more marketable and less waste-prone.

Smart Storage Solutions:

Integrating IoT (Internet of Things) technologies in storage facilities enables real-time monitoring of temperature, humidity, and other environmental factors influencing produce quality. This helps farmers maintain optimal storage conditions and reduce losses due to improper handling.

3. Access to Renewable Energy

Access to reliable, affordable, and sustainable energy is a significant challenge for rural communities. Agriculture needs energy for irrigation, processing, transportation, and storage. Rural areas often rely on expensive, polluting, and inefficient energy sources. Renewable energy technologies like solar, wind, and biogas present an opportunity to meet the energy needs of rural communities while reducing environmental impact.

A. Solar Energy for Rural Farming Communities

Solar energy is one of the most influential and accessible renewable sources for rural areas, particularly in regions with abundant sunlight. Solar power can be used in various ways to support sustainable farming.

Solar-Powered Irrigation Systems:

Solar-powered irrigation systems are increasingly used in rural farming to reduce dependence on costly and unsustainable groundwater pumping.

These systems use solar panels to power water pumps, providing farmers affordable and environmentally friendly irrigation solutions.

Solar-Powered Drying and Storage:

Solar energy can power drying systems that preserve crops by reducing their moisture content, making them less susceptible to spoilage. Solar-powered cold storage systems also help protect perishable items, thus reducing food waste.

Energy for Processing: Solar energy can also power small-scale food processing units, such as mills or grinders, allowing farmers to add value to their products without relying on costly fuel-based power.

B. Wind Energy for Rural Areas

Wind power can supplement energy needs in rural farming communities, particularly in regions with consistent wind patterns.

Wind-Powered Water Pumps:

In areas where solar energy is not as viable, wind-powered water pumps can be used for irrigation and livestock watering, reducing the need for fossil fuel-powered pumps.

Community Wind Turbines:

Small, community-based wind turbines can generate electricity for local communities, providing power for lighting, communications, and other basic needs.

C. Biogas for Rural Farming

Biogas is another renewable energy source that can help rural farmers meet their energy needs. It is produced by the anaerobic digestion of organic waste, such as crop residues, animal manure, and food waste, which are common in rural farming communities.

Biogas for Cooking and Lighting:

Biogas can be used for cooking, reducing the reliance on expensive wood, charcoal, or kerosene, which contribute to deforestation. It can also be used for lighting and improving the living conditions of rural families.

Biogas for Fertilizer Production:

The by-products of biogas production, particularly the nutrient-rich slurry, can be used as a natural fertiliser for crops, reducing the need for chemical fertilisers and improving soil health.

Author Qualifications and Honours

D.D, Doctor of Divinity

Certificate in Bible studies

Theology

Laws

(LLM)Master of Law.

Postgraduate Laws

legal research,

Business, CSR Corporate social responsibility and human Right law."

Institutional development and management,

 International Law.

BA (Hons), Laws

Law: includes Criminal, Tort, damages, Contract, Property, Equity and Trust, European Law, Public, Constitutional, Judicial Review, and Agency.

Advance Dip. Business Law, Level 4: include Employment, Agency, Damages, Tort, Contract, employment tribunal etc.

Dip. Criminology

Accounting

BA (Hons)op.

Financial Accountant

Management Accountant

Cert. Acct; (Certified accountant)

(PCA)Professional Certificate in Financial and Management Accountant

Dip. Book-keeping, Level 3

Nursing

Nursing: RMN Registered Mental Nurse)

GN (General Trained Nurse)

Lecturer qualifications

DD Doctor of Divinity

LLM Master of Laws

BA (Hons)

BSc Hons o/g)psychology with counselling

Cert. in Education (Lecturer)

Business Certificate in Advanced Management

Cert. Business Enterprise

Advanced Food Hygiene

Intermediate Health and Safety

Dip. Safety Management

International Entrepreneur for over 25 years

(NVQ); Internal Verifier, (V1)

Trainer and Assessor A1 (NVQ)

Computers

Diploma; Cisco Level 2 Technician (build, repair, networking)

Microsoft Specialist

Dip. Claire Plus (in all software)

New Clait Dip. Level 2

ECDL Level 2

Scrip writer

Diploma in scrip writing.

TV, radio, stage, and film

Diploma in writing.

Autobiography

Biography

Family History

Certificate in Poetry

Psychology and Counselling

BSc(Hons o/g) psychology with counselling

Diploma in Counselling and Psychology

Cert. in Counselling and Psychology

Certificate in Social science

Photography

Cert. (PGFP).

Portrait, Glamour and Figure

Plumbing

Level 3 City and Guild

Hypnotherapy

Dip. Hypnotherapy

Other Books by the Author James Safo

140 books.

Academic, Faith and non-faith books

Faith books- in 5 different languages :

Arabic, Chinese, English, French, Spanish

ALL FAITHS

Theology

Love All Faiths

Faith Unity

Religion And Law: religion influences National and international laws.

CHRISTIANITY

BIBLE New Testament; 1,111 QUESTIONS AND ANSWERS: Plus, synopsis and Test yourself

Bible Old Testament 1,064 Questions and Answers and Synopsis

Jesus Christ is Coming Soon

God Loves Christianity

God's/Allah's Messengers

Islam v. Christianity

Jesus Christ is Coming soon

Psychology of religion politics and marriage

Faith unity.

Faith unity simplified version.

Islamisme versus Christianism.

Love all faith.

ISLAM (In English)

QUR'AN; 1,044 Questions & Answers.

Allah Loves Islam

Islam v. Christianity

BUDDHISM (In English)

God Enlighten Buddhism

HINDUISM (In English)

Parama Nandra Loves Hindus

FREEMASON (In English)

In Search of Wisdom in Freemasonry

FRENCH BOOKS (Religious)

Allah Aimel'islam (Allah loves Islam)

Aimetouteslesfois (Love All Faiths)

Islamisme. V. christianisme (Islam v Christianity)

Dieu Aime Le Christianisme (God loves Christianity)

Les Messagers De Dieu/ Allah (God/Allah Messengers)

A LA Recherche De La Sagesse Dans La Franc - Maconnerie (In Search of wisdom)

SPANISH BOOKS (Religious)

En Busca De Le Sabiduria Masoneri (In search of wisdom in freemasonry)

Ametodas las creencias (Love All Faith)

Mensajeros de Dios (God Messengers)

4Dios Ama El Christianismo (God Loves Christianity)

Islamities v Cristianismo (Islam V Christianity)

Allah am el Islam (Allah Loves Islam)

ARABIC (Religious)

الاسلام يحب الله. . (Allah loves Islam)

الأديان جميع حب . Love All Faith

CHINESS BOOKS (Religious)

Books in Chinese

伊斯蘭教訴基督教 (Islam v Christianity)

上帝爱伊斯兰教 (Allah Loves Islam) - Traditional Chinese Edition

NON-FAITH BOOKS- IN ENGLISH LANGUAGES

LAW:

Global Injustice

The Journey to Law Graduation

THE JOURNEY TO MASTER OF LAWS

International Laws plus 30 dissertation

Laws - United Kingdom +30 dissertation

The Law (Over 1,160 Questions and Answers)

Business Law volume 1; over 800 Q&A (contract, employment, types of Human Right

Business Law Volume 2 over 600 Q&A (Tort, CSR, Equity, Trust

Criminology: (Over 1,300 Questions and Answers)

Religion And Law

POEMS

102 Poems on North America

70 Poems on South American Countries and Cities

80 POEMS ON THE ARCTIC AND ANTARCTICA

102 POEMS ON AUSTRALIA, OCEANIA, NEW ZEALAND

101 Poems on Asia countries and cities

118 USA POEMS: 50 States, Cities and Maps

114 Poems on 54 African countries

Over 200 Love Poems plus over 100 love icebreakers

Over 100 Poems on Faith & Victory

107 Poems on Discrimination, Racism & Suffering

Jesus Christ, Prophet, Arch Angels, Saint (Over 150 poems and Biography

The One - Over 130 Poems "DCF"

105 Poems on 54 European Countries & Cities

BUSINESS

Developing and Managing Institutions and Organisations Volume 1

Developing and Managing Institutions and Organisations Volume 2

Set up and manage a business

How to set up a care home and care agency

How to manage a care home and care agency

Care Home: Staff training

COMPUTER

Computing for beginners+310 questions and answers.

How to Build and Upgrade a Computer and Network

The Path of Information to the Computer Screen

Computer Programming, Coding & Science Dissertation

ACCOUNT

Financial Accounting (Over 1,241 Questions and Answers)

Management Accounting (1015 Questions & Answers Plus 100 Self-Assessment Questions)

PSYCHOLOGY

Journey to Psychology Graduation Volume 1

Journey to Psychology Graduation Volume 2

Psychology of Religion, Politics & Marriage

COUNSELLING

Journey to Counselling Graduation Volume 1

Journey to Counselling Graduation Volume 2

Counselling; Journey to Graduation Volume 3

Mood Disorder & Therapy

HISTORY

History; Journey to Graduation: 38 Essays

ENEMIES Within the earth

Slavery And Suffering

Slavery to Mastership

GEOGRAPHY

Geography: The Road to Graduation: 30 Essays

Medical/Nursing/ Health & Social

Drugs for Diseases: 1,007 Questions and Answers

Health and Social Care

Journey to Nursing Graduation: 51 Essays

Mental and Physical Diseases - Plus Nursing and 53 Dissertations

Health and Social Care - Plus 50 Dissertations

SOCIAL SCIENCE

Understanding Sociology Science - Plus 56 Dissertations

WOMEN

Women are superior to men

Sweet and Sour Women (plus over 500 love letters from women)

MANAGEMENT

Project management

RESEARCH

Research

Midwifery

A modern approach to Agriculture Introduction level, Added Value to Agriculture advanced level.

The Roadmap to sustainable agriculture in rural development.

References

Anderson, D., & Leach, M. (2001). *Environmental politics in developing countries: From policy to practice*. Routledge.

Altieri, M. A. (2002). *Agroecology: The science of sustainable agriculture*. CRC Press.

Brown, L. R. (2008). *Plan B 3.0: Mobilizing to save civilisation*. W.W. Norton & Company.

Darnhofer, I., Gibbon, D., & Dedieu, B. (2012). *Farming systems research into the 21st century: The new dynamic*. Springer.

De Schutter, O. (2011). *The right to food and the global food crisis*. Routledge.

Food and Agriculture Organization (FAO). (2017). *The future of food and agriculture: Trends and challenges*. FAO.

Food and Agriculture Organization (FAO). (2018). *The state of the world's biodiversity for food and agriculture*. FAO.

Food and Agriculture Organization (FAO) & International Fund for Agricultural Development

(IFAD). (2019). *Rural development and agriculture in the context of the sustainable development goals.* FAO & IFAD.

Fischer, G., Shah, M., & van Velthuizen, H. (2002). *Climate change and agriculture: Analysis of potential impacts and adaptation options.* Springer.

Giller, K. E., & Palmer, M. (2006). *Sustainable intensification in Sub-Saharan Africa.* Springer.

Hall, A. (2009). *Agricultural innovation in the developing world: Insights from case studies.* Springer.

International Fund for Agricultural Development (IFAD). (2017). *Rural development report 2017: Creating opportunities for rural youth.* IFAD.

Intergovernmental Panel on Climate Change (IPCC). (2014). *Climate change 2014: Impacts, adaptation, and vulnerability.* IPCC.

Klein, A. M., & Tscharntke, T. (2008). *A global perspective on sustainable agriculture and the role of agroecosystems.* Springer.

Lamers, J. P. A., & Giller, K. E. (2017). *Sustainable agriculture: A policy agenda for the future.* Elsevier.

Lipper, L., & Thornton, P. K. (2014). *Climate change, agriculture, and food security: A global perspective.* Springer.

McIntyre, B. D., Herren, H. R., Wakhungu, J., & Watson, R. T. (2009). *International assessment of agricultural knowledge, science and technology for development: Global report.* Island Press.

Milder, J. C., & Bubb, M. (2015). *Agroforestry: Enhancing sustainability in agriculture.* Springer.

O'Hara, S. U. (2013). *Rural development and the global food system: Sustainable solutions for food security.* Policy Press.

Otero, G., & Gibbons, S. (2015). *The political economy of the sustainable development goals.* Earthscan.

Pretty, J. (2008). *Sustainable agriculture: The path to food security.* Earthscan.

Pretty, J., & Bharucha, Z. P. (2014). *Sustainable intensification in agriculture.* Springer.

Robertson, G. P., & Swinton, S. M. (2005). *Sustainable agricultural systems: Managing environmental, economic, and social trade-offs.* Springer.

Ruttan, V. W. (2001). *Technology, growth, and development: An induced innovation perspective.* Oxford University Press.

Sachs, J. D. (2015). *The age of sustainable development.* Columbia University Press.

Scherr, S. J., & McNeely, J. A. (2008). *Sustainable agriculture and food security: A global perspective.* Earthscan.

Shiva, V. (2000). *Stolen harvest: The hijacking of the global food supply.* South End Press.

Smit, B., & Wandel, J. (2006). *Adaptation to climate change in agricultural systems.* Springer.
United Nations Development Programme (UNDP). (2019). *Human development report 2019: Beyond income, beyond averages, beyond today.* UNDP.

United Nations Framework Convention on Climate Change (UNFCCC). (2015). *Paris agreement on climate change.* UNFCCC.

World Bank. (2013). *Agriculture for development: Toward a new paradigm.* World Bank Publications.

World Economic Forum (2020). *The future of food: Shaping the global food system in a changing climate.* WEF.

World Trade Organization (WTO). (2015). *Trade and sustainable development: Promoting global partnerships*. WTO.

Glossary

A

Agribusiness

Agribusiness refers to the business activities involved in agriculture. It encompasses everything from farm production and processing to the distribution and marketing of agricultural products. In today's global economy, agribusiness plays a significant role in rural and urban communities. It contributes to job creation, economic growth, and food security.

Agriculture

Agriculture is cultivating crops and rearing animals for food, fibre, medicinal plants, and other products. It is the foundation of our food system and an essential industry worldwide. Agriculture has evolved over centuries with technological advancements, science, and best practices. It encompasses various sectors such as crop production, livestock management, horticulture, and agroforestry.

Agronomy

Agronomy is a branch of agricultural science that focuses on the study of crops and their cultivation. It includes various aspects such as soil management, crop rotation, irrigation methods, pest control, and plant breeding. Agronomists work closely with farmers to improve crop productivity, enhance soil health, and maximize resource efficiency. Their expertise is crucial in ensuring sustainable and profitable agricultural practices.

Aquaculture

Aquaculture is the farming of aquatic organisms, including fish, mollusks, crustaceans, and aquatic plants. It is an important sector of agriculture that provides a significant portion of the world's seafood consumption. Aquaculture involves the breeding, rearing, and harvesting of aquatic species in controlled environments such as ponds, tanks, and cages. It plays a vital role in meeting the growing demand for seafood, reducing pressure on wild fish populations, and promoting food security.

In the next section, we will explore more important terms in agriculture starting with the letter "B". Stay tuned for more insights into the fascinating world of agriculture.

B: Biotechnology

Biotechnology is a fascinating field that intersects with agriculture in many ways. It involves the use of living organisms or their parts to create or modify products, improve crops, and enhance agricultural processes. In this section, I'll delve into the various aspects of biotechnology in agriculture.

Genetic Engineering

Genetic engineering is a key aspect of biotechnology that has revolutionized agriculture. Through this technique, scientists can modify the genetic makeup of plants and animals to enhance desirable traits, such as disease resistance, higher yield, and improved nutrient content. This has opened up new possibilities for creating crops that are more resilient, productive, and nutritious.

Genetically Modified Organisms (GMOs)

Genetically modified organisms, commonly known as GMOs, are organisms whose genetic material has been altered through genetic engineering. GMOs have generated both excitement and controversy in the agricultural community. While some see them as a valuable tool in addressing food security and sustainability, others raise

213

concerns about their potential long-term effects on human health and the environment.

Biotech Crops

Biotech crops, including genetically modified crops, have gained significant traction in agriculture. According to the International Service for the Acquisition of Agri-biotech Applications (ISAAA), biotech crops were planted on over 190 million hectares worldwide in 2018. These crops offer various benefits, such as increased yields, reduced pesticide usage, and improved tolerance to harsh environmental conditions. Some commonly grown biotech crops include corn, soybeans, and cotton.

Precision Agriculture

Another application of biotechnology in agriculture is precision agriculture. This approach utilizes advanced technologies, such as drones, sensors, and GPS tracking, to gather data about soil conditions, crop health, and weather patterns. With this information, farmers can make informed decisions regarding irrigation, fertilization, and pest management, optimizing resource usage and improving crop performance.

Bioremediation

Biotechnology also plays a vital role in environmental sustainability through bioremediation. This technique uses living organisms to clean up pollutants in soil, water, and air. It has the potential to address the environmental challenges associated with agricultural activities, such as the contamination of soil and water by pesticides or the release of greenhouse gases from livestock. Bioremediation offers a greener, more sustainable approach to managing agricultural waste and reducing environmental impact.

C: Crop Rotation

Crop rotation is a fundamental practice in agriculture that involves systematically sequencing different crops on the same piece of land. As an experienced farmer, I know the immense benefits that crop rotation brings to the table. Here are a few key aspects to consider:

Crop Rotation:

- Increases soil fertility:

Crop rotation helps replenish soil nutrients by alternating the types of crops planted. Different crops have different nutrient demands, and by rotating crops, we can prevent nutrient depletion and ensure a healthy, nutrient-rich soil.

- Reduces pest and disease pressure:

- One of the significant advantages of crop rotation is its ability to break the lifecycle of pests and pathogens that can damage crops. By changing the crop types, we disrupt these pests' habitat and food sources, reducing the risk of infestations and diseases. This natural pest management practice can significantly decrease the need for chemical interventions.

- Improves soil structure: Different crops have different root structures. Some crops have deep taproots, while others have fibrous roots. When we rotate crops, we are essentially diversifying the root systems in the soil, which can help improve soil structure. This promotes better water infiltration, reduces soil erosion, and enhances overall soil health.

Cultivation:

Cultivation is an essential practice in agriculture that involves preparing the soil, planting, and caring for crops. It is a vital step in the farming process, and there are various cultivation methods that farmers can employ to maximize their yields. Let's delve into a few key points about cultivation:

- Tillage: Tillage is a common cultivation method that involves breaking up the soil to prepare it for planting. It helps with weed control, seedbed preparation, and nutrient distribution. However, excessive tillage can lead to soil erosion and loss of organic matter. Farmers are now adopting reduced tillage and no-till practices to preserve soil health and minimize environmental impact.

- Direct seeding: Direct seeding, also known as no-till or zero-tillage, is a cultivation method where seeds are planted directly into untilled soil. This method helps to conserve soil moisture, reduce erosion, and maintain soil structure. Direct seeding is gaining popularity among farmers who prioritize sustainability and want to minimize soil disturbance.

- Precision cultivation: Precision cultivation is a modern farming approach that utilizes technology to optimize the cultivation process. It involves the use of GPS-guided

217

machinery, sensors, and data analysis to precisely control seed placement, fertilizer application, and irrigation. This method allows for better resource management, reduces input wastage, and improves overall crop yields.

Crop rotation and cultivation are crucial aspects of agriculture that positively impact soil health, pest management, and crop productivity. By adopting these practices, farmers can enhance sustainability, reduce environmental impact, and ensure the long-term viability of their farms.

D: Dairy Farming

Dairy farming plays a crucial role in agriculture. As a farmer, I understand the significance of this sector and its contribution to both food production and the economy. In this section, I'll delve into various aspects of dairy farming, including its importance, challenges, and practices.

Importance of Dairy Farming

Dairy farming is essential for meeting the world's demand for milk and dairy products. It provides a steady source of nutrition, livelihood, and income for farmers and rural communities. Moreover, milk is a valuable source of essential nutrients like calcium, protein, and vitamins. With the growing population and increasing demand for dairy products, the dairy farming industry plays a vital role in food security.

Challenges in Dairy Farming

Like any other agricultural sector, dairy farming faces several challenges that need to be addressed. These challenges include:

1. Economic Uncertainty: Fluctuating milk prices and market volatility can pose challenges for dairy farmers, impacting their profitability and financial stability. It's crucial to implement effective risk management strategies to mitigate these uncertainties.

2. Animal Welfare: Ensuring the well-being and welfare of dairy cows is of utmost importance. Farmers need to provide proper housing, nutrition, and healthcare to maintain the health and productivity of their animals.

3. Environmental Sustainability: Dairy farming can have environmental impacts, such as greenhouse gas emissions, water pollution, and land degradation. Implementing sustainable practices like efficient waste

management, reducing emissions, and improving resource efficiency is essential for mitigating these effects.

Best Practices in Dairy Farming

To overcome challenges and ensure the sustainability of dairy farming, adopting best practices is vital. Here are some key practices that farmers can implement:

1. Good Herd Management: Proper monitoring of the health and productivity of dairy cows, including regular veterinary care, balanced nutrition, and appropriate breeding techniques, is crucial for maintaining a productive and healthy herd.

2. Efficient Feed Management: Balancing the nutritional needs of dairy cows with sustainable feeding practices can ensure optimal productivity and reduce the environmental impact of dairy farming. Precise feeding techniques, including ration formulation and feed quality evaluation, play a significant role in this regard.

3. Technology Adoption: Embracing technology in dairy farming can improve efficiency,

productivity, and overall farm management. Tools like automated milking systems, monitoring devices for cow health, and data analytics can help farmers make informed decisions and optimize their operations.

Erosion Control

When it comes to agriculture, Erosion Control is a critical aspect that cannot be overlooked. Erosion is the movement of soil particles by wind, water, or other forces, leading to the loss of topsoil. This can result in reduced soil fertility, impaired water quality, and decreased crop productivity.

To mitigate erosion and protect the soil, farmers employ various Erosion Control measures. Here are a few effective strategies:

Contour Plowing

Contour ploughing involves ploughing across the slope of the land, creating ridges and furrows that run parallel to the contours of the land. This helps slow the flow of water and prevent it from gaining momentum and carrying away soil particles.

Terracing

Terracing is another effective method that involves creating levelled platforms across a slope. These platforms reduce the length of the slope and create small, flat areas where water can be held and absorbed by the soil. This prevents excessive runoff and erosion.

Cover Crops

During the off-season, planting cover crops, such as rye, clover, or legumes, can significantly aid erosion control. Their root systems hold the soil in place, preventing it from being washed or blown away by the elements.

Buffer Strips

Buffer strips, also known as conservation strips, are areas of vegetation strategically planted along streams, rivers, or other water bodies. These strips act as a barrier that slows down the flow of water, traps sediment and helps control erosion.

Mulching

Mulching is the practice of covering the soil surface with a layer of organic material, such as straw, wood chips, or compost. This protective layer reduces the impact of rainfall, helps to maintain soil moisture, and prevents erosion by absorbing and holding water.

Implementing erosion control measures not only preserves the valuable topsoil but also helps to maintain soil structure, enhance crop yields, and improve overall sustainability in agriculture. By adopting these strategies, farmers can conserve soil resources and contribute to the long-term viability of their farms.

Next, let's move on to the critical topic of Fertilizer Management in agriculture.

F: Fertilizers

Fertilizers play a crucial role in ensuring the health and productivity of crops in agriculture. They are substances that provide essential nutrients to plants, helping them grow and develop to their full potential. In this section, I'll delve into the importance of fertilisers and their impact on agricultural productivity.

Fertilisers and Nutrient Balance

One key aspect of using fertilizers is maintaining a proper balance of nutrients in the soil. Different crops have varying nutrient requirements, and fertilisers help bridge the nutrient gap to ensure optimal growth. Proper nutrient management enhances crop yield and minimises nutrient deficiencies and imbalances that can hinder plant growth.

Types of Fertilizers

Fertilisers come in different forms, each designed to supply specific plant nutrients. Here are a few common types of fertilisers:

- Macronutrient-Based Fertilizers:

These fertilisers contain the essential macronutrients nitrogen (N), phosphorus (P), and potassium (K), which plants need in larger quantities. Examples include urea, diammonium phosphate (DAP), and potassium chloride (KCl).

- Micronutrient-Based Fertilizers:

Plants sometimes require trace amounts of certain micronutrients for healthy growth. Micronutrient-based fertilisers, such as iron (Fe), zinc (Zn), and manganese (Mn) fertilisers, address these specific nutrient needs.

- Organic Fertilizers:

- In addition to synthetic fertilisers, organic fertilisers are gaining popularity in agriculture. Organic fertilisers are derived from natural sources, such as compost, manure, and plant remnants. They provide essential nutrients and help improve soil health and fertility in the long run.

The Impact of Fertilizer Use

Fertilisers have significantly transformed modern agriculture, increasing crop production and higher food security. Fertilisers help maximise crop yields and contribute to global food production by providing the necessary nutrients. However, it is crucial to use fertilisers judiciously and employ sustainable practices to minimise environmental impacts, such as nutrient runoff and groundwater contamination.

H3: Food Security

Food security is a pressing issue worldwide, and agriculture plays a pivotal role in ensuring a stable food supply. In this section, I'll highlight the importance of agriculture in achieving food security and explore some key strategies to address this global challenge.

Sustainable Agriculture for Food Security

Sustainable agriculture practices are essential for long-term food security. These practices aim to optimise productivity while minimising negative environmental impacts. By adopting sustainable techniques like crop rotation, agroforestry, and conservation farming, farmers can increase resilience to climate change, protect natural resources, and ensure sustainable food production for future generations.

Technology and Innovation

Technology and innovation play crucial roles in the quest for food security. Advancements in agricultural technology, such as precision farming, genetic engineering, and remote sensing, have the potential to revolutionise food production. These tools empower farmers to make informed decisions, optimise resource allocation, and improve crop yields, contributing to global food security.

Access to Markets and Infrastructure

Ensuring access to markets and proper infrastructure is vital for attaining food security. Efficient transportation and storage facilities help reduce post-harvest losses and enable farmers to reach consumers promptly. Additionally, access to fair market prices and trade policies that support small-scale farmers can help improve their income and livelihoods, leading to enhanced food security at both the local and global levels.

Conclusion

Fertilisers are invaluable in modern agriculture, helping bridge nutrient gaps and maximize crop yields. Additionally, addressing food security demands sustainable agricultural practices, technological innovations, and improved market access. We can work towards a more secure and sustainable food future by leveraging these strategies.

G: Agriculture Words A to Z

Genetic Engineering

Genetic engineering is a revolutionary technique that has significantly impacted agriculture. It involves manipulating the genetic material of plants and animals to enhance desirable traits. Through genetic engineering, scientists can introduce genes from one organism into another, resulting in the development of genetically modified organisms (GMOs). This technique has opened up new possibilities in agriculture, enabling the creation of crops that are more resistant to pests, diseases, and environmental conditions.

Genetically Modified Organisms (GMOs)

Genetically modified organisms, or GMOs, are a hot topic in agriculture. These are living organisms whose genetic material has been altered through genetic engineering. GMOs offer several advantages for farmers, including increased crop yield, improved nutritional content, and reduced reliance on pesticides. However, GMOs have also been controversial, with concerns about their potential impact on human health and the environment. It is crucial to carefully evaluate the benefits and risks associated with GMOs and ensure that they are adequately regulated and labelled.

Greenhouse

Greenhouses are enclosed structures that provide a controlled environment for growing plants. These structures are essential for extending the growing season and protecting crops from harsh weather conditions. By trapping heat from the sun, greenhouses create a warm and stable environment that promotes optimal plant growth. They are equipped with various systems to regulate temperature, humidity, and ventilation to create ideal conditions for plants. Greenhouses allow farmers to cultivate crops unsuited to the local climate and enable year-round production of vegetables, flowers, and other plants.

Incorporating genetic engineering, genetically modified organisms (GMOs), and greenhouses into agriculture practices has revolutionized the industry. These advancements have allowed for the development of more resilient crops, increased food production, and better crop protection. However, it is crucial to balance technological advancements and environmental sustainability. By implementing responsible practices and regulations, we can harness the potential of these innovations while minimizing their potential negative impacts.

H: Harvest

Harvest is a crucial stage in agriculture, marking the culmination of hard work and dedication. During this phase, crops are gathered from the fields and prepared for further processing or consumption. Let's explore the significance of harvest and its role in ensuring food security.

Harvesting Techniques

Harvesting techniques vary depending on the type of crop and its intended use. Some common methods include:

Manual Harvesting:

This involves handpicking crops, such as fruits and vegetables, which require delicate handling to preserve their quality.

Mechanical Harvesting:

This technique employs machinery to efficiently gather large quantities of crops, particularly grains and oilseeds. It helps save time and labour, enabling farmers to harvest crops on a larger scale.

Importance of Timely Harvest

Timing is crucial when it comes to harvest. Harvesting crops at the right stage of maturity ensures optimal quality and yield. Delaying the harvest can lead to overripening, which decreases nutritional value and increases the risk of spoilage.

Conversely, premature harvesting can result in underdeveloped crops with lower yields. Hence, it is essential for farmers to monitor their crops closely and harvest at the appropriate time.

Horticulture

Horticulture is a branch of agriculture that focuses on cultivating plants for aesthetic, medicinal, and culinary purposes. It includes various sub-disciplines, such as fruit cultivation, flower production, and nursery management.

Horticulture plays a vital role in enhancing the aesthetics of urban areas, providing green spaces, and contributing to overall well-being. Additionally, it supplies us with fresh produce, medicinal herbs, and ornamental plants.

There are several essential practices in horticulture, including:

- Crop selection:

Choosing suitable crops that are well-suited to the local climate and market demand.

Soil management:

Ensuring proper soil fertility and health through composting, mulching, and soil testing.

Pest and disease management:

Using integrated pest management strategies to protect crops from pests and diseases while minimising chemical pesticides.

- Water conservation:

Implementing efficient irrigation techniques and water-saving practices to minimise water usage.

- Crop rotation:

Systematically rotating crops to maintain soil fertility and reduce the risk of pests and diseases.

The harvest stage in agriculture is critical for ensuring food security and preserving crop quality. Furthermore, horticulture plays a significant role in providing aesthetic beauty, fresh produce, and medicinal plants. By understanding the importance of both harvest and horticulture, we can appreciate the extensive efforts put forth by farmers and horticulturists to sustain our agricultural needs.

I:

Irrigation

Irrigation is a crucial aspect of agriculture that supplies water to crops to ensure their growth and development. It plays a vital role in maintaining the health and productivity of plants, especially in regions with limited rainfall or inadequate water sources. In this section, I will discuss the importance of irrigation in agriculture and explore different irrigation methods farmers use.

Importance of Irrigation

- Enhances crop yield:

Irrigation provides crops with the necessary water for photosynthesis, nutrient absorption, and overall growth. Adequate water supply through irrigation can significantly increase crop yields.

- Mitigates drought risks:

In areas prone to drought, irrigation can help farmers safeguard their crops from the adverse effects of water scarcity. By providing a stable water source, irrigation reduces crops' vulnerability to drought-related stress.

- Improves crop quality:

Proper irrigation ensures that crops receive an optimal amount of water, leading to improved quality attributes such as size, colour, texture, and taste. This is particularly important for fruits and vegetables.

Different Irrigation Methods

1. Surface Irrigation:

This traditional method involves flooding the fields with water, allowing it to soak into the soil. It is commonly used for crops grown in flat or gently sloping areas.

2. Sprinkler Irrigation:

This method involves distributing water through sprinklers or sprayers over crops. It is suitable for a wide range of crops and topographies.

3. Drip Irrigation:

In this method, water is directly supplied to the root zone of plants through a network of pipes and emitters. It is highly efficient as it minimises water loss due to evaporation or runoff.

4. Subsurface Irrigation:

This technique involves delivering water directly to the root zone of plants through buried drip lines or porous pipes. It reduces water loss and is particularly useful for water-sensitive crops.

5. Micro-Irrigation:

Micro-irrigation combines drip and sprinkler irrigation methods. It uses small, precise emitters to deliver water directly to the root zone, saving water and energy.

Each irrigation method has its advantages, and the choice depends on factors such as crop type, soil type, availability of water resources, and location. Farmers need to consider these factors when deciding which irrigation method to employ.

L:

Livestock

Livestock plays a crucial role in agriculture, providing a significant source of food, income, and livelihood for many communities worldwide. "livestock" refers to animals raised specifically to produce food, fibres, or labour. In this section, I will discuss the importance of livestock in agriculture and some key related aspects.

Livestock Farming

Livestock farming involves the rearing and management of various animals for different purposes. It includes the production of meat (such as beef, pork, or poultry), milk, eggs, and other animal-derived products. Livestock farming is an integral part of agricultural systems worldwide and contributes to food security and rural development.

Benefits of Livestock

Livestock farming offers several benefits to agriculture and society as a whole. Some of these benefits include:

Food Production:

Livestock farming is crucial in meeting the global demand for animal protein. It provides a significant meat, milk, and eggs source, essential to a balanced diet.

Income and Livelihood:

Livestock farming provides farmers and rural communities opportunities to generate income and improve their livelihoods. It serves as a source of employment and economic stability for many households.

- Nutrient Cycling:

Livestock converts agricultural by-products and waste materials into valuable resources. For example, cattle can graze on grasslands and convert the plant biomass into nutrient-rich manure, which can be used as organic fertiliser for crop production.

- Diversification and Risk Management:

Raising different types of livestock can help farmers diversify their income sources and manage risks associated with weather, market fluctuations, and crop failure.

Sustainable Livestock Farming

While livestock farming offers many benefits, it is crucial to ensure sustainability by adopting responsible and ethical practices. Sustainable livestock farming minimises adverse environmental impacts, promotes animal welfare, and maintains the industry's long-term viability.

Some fundamental principles of sustainable livestock farming include:

Efficient Resource Use:

Optimal utilisation of feed resources, water, and land to minimise waste and maximise productivity.

Environmental Stewardship:

Implementing practices that minimise water pollution, soil erosion, and GHG emissions, such as proper manure management and sustainable grazing practices.

Animal Welfare:

 Ensuring the well-being of animals through proper housing, healthcare, and handling practices.

Pest Control

Regarding agriculture, pest control plays a crucial role in ensuring the health and productivity of crops. As an experienced expert blogger in agriculture, I have come across various methods and techniques used for pest control. Here are some key points to consider:

Integrated Pest Management (IPM)

Integrated Pest Management is a holistic approach to pest control that focuses on minimising chemicals and maximising natural pest control methods. With

IPM, farmers aim to prevent and manage pests by employing a combination of measures such as:

Biological control methods use natural enemies of pests to control their population.

Cultural practices, such as crop rotation and intercropping, disrupt pest life cycles and create unfavourable conditions for pests.

Mechanical methods, including traps and barriers, to physically remove or deter pests.

Chemical control is a last resort, using pesticides only when necessary and choosing environmentally friendly options.

Biotechnology in Pest Control

Another aspect of pest control in agriculture is biotechnology and genetic engineering. Through genetic modification, scientists have developed crops that are resistant to pests. This technology has significantly reduced the need for chemical pesticides, making agriculture more sustainable and environmentally friendly.

Plant Breeding

Plant breeding is a vital agricultural practice that focuses on developing and improving plant varieties to enhance their traits, such as yield, disease resistance, and adaptability. As I delve into agriculture from A to Z, plant breeding is an essential aspect to cover. Here are a few key points:

Traditional Plant Breeding: For centuries, farmers and plant breeders have used traditional breeding techniques to select and cross-pollinate plants with desired traits. This process involves carefully selecting parent plants and creating offspring with improved characteristics.

Modern Plant Breeding Techniques: Modern plant breeding techniques have emerged with technological advancements. These include marker-assisted selection techniques, which allow breeders to select plants with specific genes or traits more efficiently.

Genetically Modified Organisms (GMOs): Genetic engineering techniques have also led to the development of genetically modified crops. These crops have been genetically altered to possess desired traits, such as insect resistance or herbicide tolerance.

Precision Agriculture

Precision agriculture is a modern approach that utilises technology to optimise the efficiency and sustainability of agricultural practices. It involves using GPS, drones, and remote sensing to collect data and make informed decisions. Here are a few key points to consider:

Variable Rate Technology (VRT): Precision agriculture allows farmers to apply fertilisers, pesticides, and water at variable rates based on the specific needs of different areas within a field. This targeted approach minimises waste and optimises resource usage.

Remote Sensing and Imaging: Drones equipped with cameras and sensors can capture detailed imagery and data about crops, helping farmers monitor their health, detect disease or nutrient deficiencies, and make timely interventions.

Data Analytics and Decision Support Systems: Precision agriculture relies on data analysis and decision support systems to process the collected information and provide farmers with actionable insights. This allows for precision in crop management, leading to improved yields and reduced environmental impact.

R:

Rural Development

Rural development plays a crucial role in the agricultural sector. Improving rural areas benefits the local communities and significantly impacts agricultural productivity and sustainability. In this section, I'll delve into the importance of rural development and examine some of its key aspects.

Infrastructure Development

One key pillar of rural development is improving infrastructure. When rural areas have adequate infrastructure, it becomes easier to access markets, transport goods, and connect with different parts of the country. This is particularly important in agriculture, enabling farmers to distribute their produce and access essential resources efficiently.

Infrastructure improvements can include the construction of roads, bridges, and transportation networks, as well as the development of irrigation systems and storage facilities. By investing in infrastructure, rural areas can overcome logistical challenges, reduce post-harvest losses, and improve agricultural productivity.

Access to Education and Training

Access to quality education and training is essential for rural communities to thrive. When people in rural areas have access to education, they can acquire the necessary knowledge and skills to participate effectively in the agricultural industry. This includes learning about modern farming techniques, sustainable practices, crop management, and livestock rearing, among other things.

Rural development initiatives that focus on education and training can help farmers adopt more efficient and sustainable cultivation methods. This improves their livelihoods and benefits the environment by reducing the negative impact of certain agricultural practices. Additionally, education can foster innovation and entrepreneurship in rural areas, encouraging new ideas and solutions of farming challenges.

Diversification and Value Addition

Another crucial aspect of rural development is promoting agricultural diversification and value addition. By encouraging farmers to diversify their crops and engage in value-added activities, rural areas can become less reliant on single commodities and create more diverse income streams. This reduces farmers' vulnerability to market fluctuations and increases their economic resilience.

Diversification can involve growing various crops and incorporating livestock farming into agricultural systems. It can also include the development of agro-processing and value-added industries, such as food processing, packaging, and marketing. By adding value to their products, farmers can command higher prices and increase profitability, contributing positively to rural development.

S:

Soil Conservation

Soil conservation is a crucial aspect of agriculture that focuses on protecting and preserving soil health for sustainable productivity. It involves implementing practices that reduce soil erosion, improve soil structure, and enhance nutrient content. Let me provide you with some essential information about soil conservation in agriculture:

Soil Erosion:

Soil erosion is a significant challenge in agriculture that leads to the loss of fertile topsoil, reduced water-holding capacity, and diminished soil fertility. To combat erosion, farmers and landowners employ various conservation techniques, such as:

Terracing:

Creating level platforms on steep slopes to slow water runoff and prevent soil erosion.

Contour farming:

Planting crops parallel to the land's contours minimises water flow and erosion.

Cover cropping:

Planting covers crops, like legumes or grasses, and protects the soil from erosion between main crops.

Soil Quality Improvement:

Maintaining healthy soil is essential for sustainable agriculture. Here are a few practices that help improve soil quality:

Organic matter addition:

Adding organic materials, such as compost or manure, to the soil improves its structure, nutrient content, and water-holding capacity.

Crop rotation:

 Alternating different crop species on the same land helps prevent nutrient depletion, reduces pest and disease buildup, and enhances soil fertility.

Conservation tillage:

Adopting minimum or no-till farming practices minimises soil disturbance, retains organic matter, and reduces erosion.

Sustainable Agriculture:

Sustainable agriculture is a holistic approach that aims to meet the needs of the present without compromising the ability of future generations to meet their own needs. Integrating various practices to achieve environmental, social, and economic sustainability. Critical aspects of sustainable agriculture include:

Crop diversification:

Growing various crops reduces the risk of crop failure and enhances ecosystem resilience.

Integrated nutrient management:

Efficient use of fertilisers and organic sources minimises nutrient losses and maintains soil fertility.

Water conservation:

 It was implementing irrigation techniques that maximise water efficiency and minimise usage.

Integrated pest management:

Using biological, cultural, and chemical methods to manage pests while minimising environmental impact.

By practising soil conservation and adopting sustainable agriculture techniques, we can ensure the long-term productivity of agricultural land, safeguard the environment, and contribute to a more sustainable future.

V.

Vertical Farming

An innovative and exciting concept is gaining momentum in agriculture: Vertical Farming. As the name suggests, it involves growing crops in vertical stacks or layers, creating a towering structure that maximises space utilisation. With urbanisation on the rise and limited land availability, vertical farming offers a solution to meet the increasing demand for food while conserving resources and reducing the ecological footprint.

The Benefits of Vertical Farming

Vertical farming brings a range of benefits that make it an attractive option for sustainable agriculture:

Higher Crop Yield:

Using vertical space, farmers can produce more crops per square foot than traditional farming methods. This increased yield can help meet the growing demands for food in a rapidly growing population.

Year-Round Production:

Controlled indoor environments in vertical farms allow for year-round production, eliminating the limitations of seasonal availability. This ensures a consistent fresh produce supply regardless of the external climate conditions.

Reduced Water Usage:

Vertical farming systems implemented with hydroponics or aeroponics use less water than conventional farming. Water is recycled within the system, reducing water loss through evaporation and runoff.

Minimised Pesticide Use:

In a closed and controlled environment, pests and diseases can be managed effectively, reducing the need for pesticides. This promotes healthier and more sustainable crop production.

Locally Sourced and Reduced

Transportation:

Vertical farms can be established in urban areas, bringing the production closer to the consumers. This reduces the need to transport food long distances, resulting in fresher produce and a smaller carbon footprint.

1. Land Conservation and Space Efficiency:

Vertical farming allows for the cultivation of crops in areas with limited arable land. By stacking crops vertically, more food can be grown in a smaller footprint, making it suitable for urban environments and areas with high population densities.

The Future of Agriculture

Vertical farming has the potential to revolutionise the way we produce food. With technological advancements and the increasing demand for sustainable practices, its popularity is expected to grow. This farming method is gaining traction worldwide by transforming abandoned warehouses, repurposing shipping containers, or constructing purpose-built vertical farms.

W:

Water Management

Water management is crucial in agriculture, ensuring crops receive the necessary water for healthy growth and optimal yield. As a farmer, I understand the importance of efficient water use and its impact on crop productivity. Let us delve into some key aspects of water management in agriculture:

Efficient Irrigation Practices

One of the critical components of water management in agriculture is implementing efficient irrigation practices. This involves using irrigation methods that minimise water loss and deliver water directly to the plant's root zones. Some standard techniques include:

Drip irrigation:

This method provides water directly to the roots of plants, minimising evaporation and ensuring efficient water use.

Sprinkler irrigation:

Sprinklers distribute water over a wide area, simulating rainfall and reducing water loss through evaporation.

Water Conservation Strategies

Sustainable water management also involves adopting various conservation strategies to minimise water waste. By implementing these practices, we can effectively reduce our water footprint and contribute to conserving this precious resource.

Here are some effective water conservation strategies used in agriculture:

Mulching:

Applying a layer of mulch around plants helps reduce evaporation and maintain soil moisture levels.

Crop rotation:

Rotating crops helps break disease cycles and reduces water usage by diversifying water requirements.

Cover cropping:

Planting cover crops helps improve soil structure, reduce erosion, and increase water infiltration rates.

Water Quality and Monitoring

Ensuring that water used for irrigation is of good quality is essential for crop health and productivity. Monitoring water quality helps identify potential issues that could negatively impact plant growth. As part of water management, frequent testing is crucial to maintain optimal growing conditions. Factors to consider for water quality monitoring include pH levels, salinity, and the presence of contaminants.

Rainwater Harvesting

Rainwater harvesting is another effective water management technique for agriculture. Farmers can reduce reliance on external water sources and better use natural resources by collecting and storing rainfall for later use. Rainwater harvesting is particularly beneficial in regions with limited water availability and unreliable rainfall patterns.

Conclusion

Water management is an essential aspect of agriculture, and implementing effective strategies can help ensure the sustainable use of this valuable resource. By adopting efficient irrigation practices, conserving water, monitoring water quality, and exploring rainwater harvesting, farmers can optimise their water use and contribute to a more sustainable and resilient agricultural system.

INDEX

agriculture, 2, 3, 6, 18, 19, 20, 21, 22, 23, 24, 26, 29, 32, 33, 36, 38, 42, 52, 59, 60, 62, 63, 72, 79, 81, 84, 88, 91, 92, 94, 95, 97, 98, 103, 106, 108, 109, 110, 112, 113, 114, 116, 117, 118, 119, 120, 121, 122, 123, 124, 125, 127, 128, 129, 130, 131, 132, 135, 141, 145, 154, 156, 157, 158, 159, 160, 161, 162, 163, 164, 165, 166, 167, 168, 169, 170, 171, 173, 174, 175, 176, 177, 178, 179, 181, 183, 191, 196, 219, 220, 221, 222, 223, 225, 226, 227, 228, 229, 231, 232, 233, 236, 238, 240, 241, 242, 243, 244, 245, 246, 248, 251, 252, 254, 255, 256, 257, 258, 261, 262, 263, 264, 265, 267, 268, 270

agroforestry, 20, 24, 46, 47, 88, 104, 119, 126, 127, 141, 142, 143, 144, 145, 174, 178, 184, 225, 241

Bridging, 16, 194

building, 3, 183

Climate, 2, 12, 13, 24, 84, 86, 89, 90, 94, 109, 117, 126, 131, 142, 164, 168, 171, 178, 181, 193, 221, 222, 224

Crop, 10, 11, 12, 20, 26, 39, 40, 52, 55, 56, 57, 62, 65, 67, 68, 72, 76, 88, 89, 95, 229, 230, 232, 247, 248, 262, 263, 265, 269

directions, 3

economic, 3, 6, 18, 21, 22, 23, 43, 47, 77, 97, 98, 100, 101, 103, 105, 108, 109, 110, 112, 116, 123, 125, 133, 154, 156, 161, 166, 167, 174, 176, 183, 194, 196, 200, 223, 225, 252, 260, 263

energy, 21, 31, 76, 93, 99, 102, 135, 196, 204, 205, 206, 207, 250

environmental, 6, 18, 21, 22, 23, 29, 30, 32, 33, 36, 39, 42, 45, 46, 61, 63, 64, 68, 72, 75, 76, 77, 78, 81, 82, 94, 97, 98, 103, 105, 112, 116, 117, 119, 120, 125, 126, 129, 132, 133, 143, 144, 146, 147, 148, 149, 150, 151, 156, 157, 165, 167, 169, 170, 172, 173, 174, 179, 180, 203, 204, 223, 228, 229, 232, 233, 234, 235, 241, 243, 245, 253, 258, 263, 264

Farming, 6, 10, 11, 12, 13, 14, 17, 31, 35, 42, 55, 64, 67, 98, 104, 122, 138, 158, 204, 207, 220,

233, 234, 235, 251, 253,
264, 265
food, 6, 7, 18, 20, 22, 32,
36, 39, 43, 54, 56, 58,
72, 77, 78, 84, 86, 89,
96, 97, 116, 117, 118,
125, 130, 131, 132, 156,
158, 160, 161, 163, 167,
170, 172, 174, 176, 177,
179, 180, 199, 200, 203,
205, 207, 220, 222, 223,
224, 225, 226, 228, 230,
233, 234, 240, 241, 242,
245, 248, 251, 252, 260,
264, 265, 266, 267
God, 5
governance, 3
health, 18, 19, 22, 27, 30,
32, 33, 39, 41, 42, 48,
52, 56, 60, 64, 65, 66,
68, 70, 75, 89, 90, 92,
95, 103, 119, 126, 128,
132, 138, 141, 149, 159,
165, 166, 175, 186, 207,
226, 228, 229, 231, 232,
233, 234, 235, 236, 238,
240, 244, 247, 248, 254,
257, 261, 269
history, 26
innovations, 2, 7, 59, 81,
82, 157, 187, 198, 242,
245
jobs, 23
land, 6, 7, 31, 35, 41, 47,
58, 77, 91, 94, 96, 116,
117, 120, 126, 128, 129,
134, 142, 143, 145, 146,
148, 150, 151, 158, 171,

175, 176, 177, 179, 230,
234, 236, 253, 262, 264,
266
Livestock, 11, 55, 56, 57,
95, 251, 252, 253
management, 2, 9, 20, 32,
36, 42, 46, 60, 61, 67,
68, 70, 72, 89, 91, 92,
95, 98, 99, 117, 119,
123, 124, 126, 129, 134,
144, 148, 149, 151, 159,
164, 165, 166, 174, 176,
177, 178, 179, 181, 184,
185, 186, 189, 199, 208,
219, 225, 226, 229, 230,
232, 233, 234, 235, 236,
239, 247, 251, 254, 258,
259, 263, 264, 267, 268,
269, 270
natural, 6, 18, 19, 23, 26,
27, 29, 41, 42, 44, 45,
46, 50, 57, 59, 73, 95,
98, 120, 138, 140, 159,
180, 207, 230, 240, 241,
254, 255, 270
nutrition, 22, 171, 233,
234, 235
organic, 27, 30, 32, 33, 34,
38, 42, 43, 48, 54, 55,
56, 78, 90, 92, 93, 98,
99, 100, 102, 103, 105,
106, 108, 109, 110, 118,
119, 126, 127, 132, 133,
134, 137, 139, 142, 145,
152, 161, 166, 174, 178,
180, 181, 207, 231, 238,
240, 253, 262, 263

practices, 2, 3, 19, 20, 21,
22, 23, 24, 26, 29, 30,
31, 32, 33, 34, 36, 37,
39, 42, 46, 50, 62, 71,
72, 75, 79, 82, 84, 87,
88, 89, 90, 91, 93, 94,
97, 98, 99, 100, 101,
102, 103, 104, 105, 106,
108, 109, 110, 112, 113,
114, 116, 117, 119, 120,
121, 122, 123, 124,125,
126, 127, 128, 129, 130,
131, 133, 134, 136, 140,
141, 143, 145, 146, 148,
149, 150, 152, 153, 154,
156, 157, 159, 160, 161,
162, 163, 164, 165, 166,
167, 168, 170, 171, 173,
175, 176, 177, 178, 179,
180, 181, 183, 184, 186,
187, 189, 190, 225, 226,
232, 233, 235, 240, 241,
242, 244, 247, 248, 253,
254, 255, 257, 259, 261,
262, 263, 267, 268, 270
rural, 2, 3, 6, 7, 20, 22, 23,
24, 32, 46, 47, 49, 50,
52, 53, 54, 55, 56, 58,
59, 69, 72, 78, 80, 81,
84, 86, 97, 101, 102,

105, 110, 115, 117, 118,
122, 125, 126, 127, 129,
130, 131, 135, 136, 140,
145, 156, 157, 161, 162,
164, 166, 167, 169, 179,
180, 183, 184, 185, 186,
188, 189, 191, 192, 193,
194, 196, 197, 198, 200,
202, 204, 205, 206, 207,
219, 221, 225, 233, 252,
258, 259, 260
Social, 3, 12, 20, 24, 78,
114, 166, 167, 210, 218
soil,, 21, 27, 34, 35, 40, 42,
43, 47, 68, 229, 231, 236
traditional, 21, 26, 29, 31,
38, 63, 94, 112, 119,
120, 121, 140, 190, 198,
250, 256, 265
universities, 123, 136,
154, 184
viability, 3, 18, 43, 97, 101,
103, 108, 109, 110, 167,
200, 233, 238, 253
Waste, 21
Water, 2, 10, 27, 36, 38,
54, 89, 90, 139, 165,
206, 247, 263, 265, 267,
268, 269, 270
Youth, 13, 122, 123, 124

www.ingramcontent.com/pod-product-compliance
Lightning Source LLC
Chambersburg PA
CBHW070350200326
41518CB00012B/2194